Books in Motion

Connecting Preschoolers with Books through Art, Games,
Movement, Music, Playacting, and Props

Julie Dietzel-Glair

Neal-Schuman

An imprint of the American Library Association

Chicago 2013

Julie Dietzel-Glair is a freelance writer and library consultant. She was a children's librarian in public libraries in Maryland for eleven years. Storytimes were always her favorite part of being a children's librarian. There is something magical about reading a good book and acting silly in front of a group of enthusiastic children.

Ms. Dietzel-Glair is active in the Association for Library Service to Children and has served on the John Newbery Medal Selection Committee. She is also a past president of the Children's Services Division of the Maryland Library Association and served on the Maryland Blue Crab Young Reader Award Committee.

© 2013 by the American Library Association. Any claim of copyright is subject to applicable limitations and exceptions, such as rights of fair use and library copying pursuant to Sections 107 and 108 of the U.S. Copyright Act. No copyright is claimed for content in the public domain, such as works of the U.S. government.

Printed in the United States of America
17 16 15 14 13   5 4 3 2 1

Extensive effort has gone into ensuring the reliability of the information in this book; however, the publisher makes no warranty, express or implied, with respect to the material contained herein.

ISBNs: 978-1-55570-810-8 (paper); 978-1-55570-856-6 (PDF)

Library of Congress Cataloging-in-Publication Data

Dietzel-Glair, Julie, 1976- author.
    Books in Motion : Connecting Preschoolers with Books through Art, Games, Movement, Music, Playacting, and Props / Julie Dietzel-Glair.
        pages   cm
    Includes bibliographical references and index.
    ISBN 978-1-55570-810-8
    1. Preschool children—Books and reading. 2. Children's libraries—Activity programs. 3. Public libraries—Activity programs. 4. Libraries and preschool children. 5. Readiness for school. 6. Education, Preschool—Activity programs. I. Title.
Z718.3.D54 2013
027.62'5—dc23
                                                                                                2012040993

Cover design by Rosemary Holderby/Cole Design and Production.
Text design by Kimberly Thornton in Helvetica Neue and Minion Pro.

♾ This paper meets the requirements of ANSI/NISO Z39.48-1992 (Permanence of Paper).

contents

preface / v

preface

This book is designed for children's librarians, early literacy teachers, day care providers, and anyone looking for ways to get kids up and moving during a preschool storytime. You probably already use rhymes and songs *in between* the featured books of your programs; in the pages that follow, I show you new and exciting ways to get kids moving *during* the books in your storytime.

Storytime is a fun and magical experience for children. With *Books in Motion* you can add even more excitement to your programs. Kids learn in many different ways. Some kids learn best by sitting quietly and listening, some through movement, some through music, and some through artistic expression. Elementary, middle, and high schools, as well as adult training sessions, often include multiple intelligence philosophies in their classes. The concept that everyone learns best by one, or a combination, of eight different intelligences can be included in storytimes as well. Librarians have always been able to connect with linguistic and spatial learners in picture book storytimes. Most of the other six intelligences (logical-mathematical, bodily-kinesthetic, musical, interpersonal, intrapersonal, and naturalistic) are touched upon with rhymes, songs, and crafts in between storytime books or at the end of the program. By including art, games, movement, music, playacting, and props during your storytime books, you have an even better chance of reaching all the kids in your program. As an added bonus, your storytimes will be new and exciting for kids, caregivers, and you. You already know how to do storytimes; now use *Books in Motion* to get ideas to enhance your current programming.

I have reviewed picture books published in the year 2000 and later. There are many wonderful books published before 2000, but I wanted to include books that have a higher chance of being in your collection. I have chosen what I believe to be the best 500 books with a strong movement tie-in for the preschool (three- to five-year-old) crowd. This is based on my own expertise in doing storytimes for the past eleven years. I then split the books into six possible types of movement: art, games, movement, music, playacting, and props. For each book, I provide simple instructions for including movement while you are reading the book. Some of the instructions are only two sentences long, while others require a bit more detail. All of them are straightforward and easy to include in your current storytimes.

In the first chapter, "Art," you will find books that present the option for a simple art or craft activity. Oftentimes, librarians wait until the end of storytime to do a craft. Why not try something during the books? Chapter 1 has simple coloring sheets that correspond with the books (e.g., winter wonderlands made from cotton balls) and ideas on ways to create art just like the character in the story you are reading. Where an activity calls for a simple outline to be handed out to the children, you will find the corresponding outline in the "Art Outlines" appendix at the end of *Books in Motion*. Feel free to copy and enlarge any of the images as needed. All of the art activities require little to no adult supervision and use easy-to-find supplies such as crayons, construction paper, cotton balls, and glue sticks. Remember that three- to five-year-old children can be very creative in their interpretation of a craft activity and everyone's finished product may look very different. Add to the fun by asking kids to share their beautiful artwork with the group after the story is done.

In Chapter 2, "Games," you will find games that can be played during a book. For example, when a character is searching for her favorite teddy bear, the kids can search for a teddy bear in your storytime space. Of course, this activity could wait until after the story is done, but why not stop reading for a moment so everyone can search along with the character? There are also simple follow-the-leader and guessing games. The plan is to make the book even more memorable by including the children in the story.

Get ready to jump, stomp, clap, chomp, waddle, parade, wiggle, and stretch in Chapter 3, "Movement." Some books are perfect for one simple motion throughout. If a book is about food, you can rub your stomach every time a new food is mentioned. In a frog book, you can jump like a frog every time the frog is on the page. Sometimes a book is ideal for a bunch of different motions. For example, when a book includes many forms of transportation, you can pretend to be a plane, train, car, or truck while reading about them on the pages of the book.

In Chapter 4, "Music," there are books that are perfect for being read with music, songs, or musical instruments. Many books have rhythmic language and you can shake a maraca along with the words. Some books are about dance and you can play music so everyone can dance in between pages. Other books are so full of sounds that it makes sense to add your own sounds to the text. Don't worry if you don't have bells, shakers, rhythm sticks, and drums. I may suggest a particular instrument in the directions, but you can use whatever child-friendly instruments you have in your library and let the books come to life.

In "Playacting," Chapter 5, the characters in the books are involved in a lot of activities. Kids can pretend to wash their faces, swim with fish, and fly like airplanes along with the book's protagonist. I have included instructions on how to do the different motions. For example, when the character jumps out of bed, you can jump in place. When the character cleans out a bowl, you can cup one hand into a bowl shape and pretend to wash it out with the other hand. Some books have motions that can be done on every page; sometimes there is more than one motion per page. I have included as much instruction as possible for as many motions as possible. You can do everything or pick and choose the amount of movement that is right for your storytime crowd or your personal silliness level.

Finally, bring out your puppets, flannel-board pieces, and scarves for the last chapter, "Props." Most of the books chosen have enough props for everyone in the program to have a part. Scarves can blow in the wind, be washcloths, or turn anyone into a superhero with a cape. Yellow felt stars can turn a flannel board into a starry sky. If you have a die-cut machine, you can create a paper fly for every child that they can shoo away. Even a box of tissues can add to a storytime. If you don't have the puppets or die-cut shape for a particular animal, you can always print an image from the Internet for kids to use. Don't worry if your flannel-board pieces aren't museum quality; kids will play along even if your pig looks more like a cow.

The books in each chapter are listed alphabetically by the author's last name. There is a short summary for each book followed by a description of how to include action while reading that book in storytime. For quick reference, the book includes three indexes—one by author, one by book title, and one by storytime theme.

Books in Motion: Connecting Preschoolers with Books through Art, Games, Movement, Music, Playacting, and Props concludes with two resource appendixes, "More Storytime Resources" and "Art Outlines," should you discover that you've caught the interactive storytime bug. The first provides a list and description of some other books with rhyme, song, craft, and book ideas, and the second is a handy image section that provides, as already noted, the outlines mentioned in some of the book's activities.

Some of these activities may take more time than you would usually devote to a book to complete it. Some may even use half or more of your storytime. My point is to offer you multiple ways to make books enjoyable, memorable, and exciting for the kids in your program.

Does every book in your storytime need to include movement? No. You can use one or more of these ideas as they fit into your current programming. The goal is to make the books more memorable for the kids in your programs. Once you become more confident, you may want to try a storytime built completely around movement. So, go ahead, use these ideas and create your own. Most important, have fun and make sure to keep your copy of *Books in Motion* close by so you can have exciting and movement-filled storytimes in your library.

art

Crayons and glue sticks! Children love creating art based on what they know and learn. Use the books and ideas in this chapter to help the kids in your programs use their creative energy while you read the book to them. Follow along with the artist in the book or draw a picture of the main character using common supplies such as crayons, cotton balls, and construction paper. Photocopy and enlarge the images provided in the "Art Outlines" appendix when an activity calls for a simple outline. Remember that many children enjoy sharing their work with others (which must be why refrigerator magnets were invented) and leave time at the end of your program for those who wish to present their creations.

tips

- Encourage the adults in the room to assist their children with the art activity. Consider handing out supplies to the adults so they can make their own creations.
- Consider modeling the recommended activity before reading the book. For example, if you are asking the kids to trace their hands on pieces of paper, demonstrate how to do this by holding your hand up to a piece of

paper on the flannel board. After showing them how to do the activity, read the book and let them make their creations.

- Have a sample available for kids to copy if you are asking them to have a particular end result. Hang this sample from your flannel board so all kids can see it while you read the book.

- When possible, do the art activity along with the audience. For example, if you are coloring parts of the body to match *I Ain't Gonna Paint No More!*, have a piece of paper on your flannel board so you can do the activity, too.

- Do art books at the end of storytime if your programs tend to have a large attendance in order to facilitate distribution of supplies. You can also plan to do these activities last until your group is accustomed to doing art during a story.

- Collect pieces of cardboard to hand out to the children with paper and crayons if your storytime floor is not hard enough to be conducive to coloring against the floor.

- All of these activities can be done with preschool children. If your audience is on the younger side, consider doing the simpler activities with them (i.e., simple coloring pages). As your group gets more accustomed to doing art activities in storytime, you will be able to add the more difficult crafts to your programs. You can also consider doing part of the activity in advance for them. For example, when reading *Library Lion,* hand out paper plates that already have yarn manes glued onto them. Younger children will still enjoy coloring the face on the lion.

- Some preschool children need help learning their colors. If you are asking them to color with a particular crayon, stop reading for a moment while you ask the children to hold up their red crayons (or whatever color applies). Once everyone is holding up the right crayon, continue with the activity.

- Many kids will be very proud of their creations. Be sure to leave some time for sharing.

- Be sure to include clean-up time after the art book/activity is complete. Many children love helping you putting crayons and other supplies away to a fun clean-up song.

- Remember that it is not important for the end results to look exactly as you intended. What is important is that the children have fun interacting with art and a book.

Alexander, Martha. *I'll Never Share You, Blackboard Bear.*

2003. Cambridge, MA: Candlewick Press.

Summary: Anthony finds a way to share his special blackboard bear with his friends.

Action: Give everyone a blank piece of paper and some crayons. Have the kids draw their own blackboard bears while listening to the story.

Ashman, Linda. *Castles, Caves, and Honeycombs.*

2001. Illus., Lauren Stringer. Orlando: Harcourt.

Summary: Many different types of homes are shown.

Action: Give the kids paper and crayons at the beginning of the story. As you read, let them draw a picture of their ideal homes. After the story is done invite them to share.

Baek, Matthew J. *Panda and Polar Bear.*

2009. New York: Dial Books for Young Readers.

Summary: A young panda bear and polar bear meet accidentally, yet have lots of fun together.

Action: Give the kids a piece of paper with the outline of a bear. As you read the story, let them color their own panda bears or any other type of bear.

Balan, Bruce. *Cows Going Past.*

2005. Illus., Scott Nash. New York: Dial Books for Young Readers.

Summary: While going on a car trip, the family passes many colors of cows doing a variety of activities.

Action: Give the kids a piece of a paper with an outline of a cow. As you read the story, let them color the cows they would like to see on their car trip.

Bang, Molly. *In My Heart.*

2006. New York: Little, Brown.

Summary: A parent tells a child that he is in the parent's heart all day long.

Action: Give the kids a piece of paper with an outline of a heart. As you read the story, have them draw someone or something that they love.

Bartoletti, Susan Campbell. *Nobody's Nosier Than a Cat.*

2003. Illus., Beppe Giacobbe. New York: Hyperion Books for Children.

———. *Nobody's Diggier Than a Dog.*

2005. *Illus., Beppe Giacobbe. New York: Hyperion Books for Children.*

> **Summary:** Each book humorously describes dogs/cats through many adjectives.
>
> **Action:** Give each child a piece of paper with the outline of a dog or cat and some crayons and let them color as you read the story. Or, give each child a blank piece of paper so they can draw their own dogs or cats as you read.

Barton, Byron. *My Car.*

2001. *New York: Greenwillow Books.*

> **Summary:** Sam describes how he takes care of his car and drives carefully.
>
> **Action:** Give each child a blank piece of paper and crayons. Let them draw a picture of their cars while you read the story.

Bauer, Marion Dane. *If Frogs Made Weather.*

2005. *Illus., Dorothy Donohue. New York: Holiday House.*

> **Summary:** Short descriptions of what weather would be like if different animals controlled it.
>
> **Action:** Give each child a blank piece of paper. Tell them to draw a picture of their favorite kind of day: Is it sunny? Rainy? Snowy? Read the story aloud as they draw.

Beaumont, Karen. *I Ain't Gonna Paint No More!*

2005. *Illus., David Catrow. Orlando: Harcourt.*

> **Summary:** A child paints every part of his body.
>
> **Action:** Give each child a piece of paper with two outlines of the body—one front and one back. You can use the same outline for each and simply add eyes and a mouth to the front image. Also give the children some crayons so they can color along with the book. As you get to each body part, have them color that part on their paper. You may need to wait a couple of minutes in between pages to let them find the part and color it.

Bell, Cece. *Itty Bitty.*

2009. *Somerville, MA: Candlewick Press.*

> **Summary:** An itty bitty dog creates a home out of a big bone.
>
> **Action:** Give each child some crayons and a paper with an outline of a bone. While you read the story, have them draw how they would make the bone their home.

Billstrom, Dianne. *You Can't Go to School Naked!*

2008. Illus., Don Kilpatrick III. New York: G. P. Putnam's Sons.

Summary: Parents tell their son all the reasons he can't go to school naked.

Action: Give each child some crayons and a piece of paper with the outline of a body. While you read the story, they can draw the clothes they would want to wear to school onto the person. At the end of the story, let them share their drawings.

Blabey, Aaron. *Pearl Barley and Charlie Parsley.*

2007. Asheville, NC: Front Street.

Summary: Pearl Barley and Charlie Parsley are different in so many ways yet they are really great friends.

Action: Give each child a blank piece of paper and some crayons. While you read the story, ask them to draw pictures of their best friends.

Bond, Rebecca. *This Place in the Snow.*

2004. New York: Dutton Children's Books.

Summary: After a snowfall, a group of children build a snow kingdom.

Action: Give each child some crayons, a glue stick, a few cotton balls, and a piece of paper. As you read the story, let them create their own snow kingdoms.

Brenner, Barbara. *Good Morning, Garden.*

2004. Illus., Denise Ortakales. Chanhassen, MN: NorthWord Press.

Summary: A young girl greets the plants and animals in a garden.

Action: Give each child some crayons, a glue stick, some scrap construction paper, and a piece of paper. As you read the story, have them each create a lovely garden. This would be perfect for a Mother's Day storytime because the kids would have a gift for their mothers.

Browne, Anthony. *My Dad.*

2000. New York: Farrar Straus Giroux.

———. *My Mom.*

2005. New York: Farrar Straus Giroux.

Summary: A tribute to all the wonderful things dads/moms can do.

Action: Give each child some crayons and a blank piece of paper. As you read the story, have them draw pictures of their dads or moms.

Carter, David A. *Woof! Woof!*

2006. New York: Little Simon.

Summary: Shapes cut out of the pages create a dog shape.

Action: Give each child a blank piece of paper and a crayon. When you get to the page that says "legs," have them draw some small legs on their papers. Continue having them add to their drawings as the image in the book grows. Compare their drawings with the end result of the book. This is a rather abstract book and it is probably best with your older preschool kids.

Christelow, Eileen. *Five Little Monkeys Wash the Car.*

2000. New York: Clarion Books.

Summary: While Mama sleeps, five little monkeys clean, paint, and sell their old car.

Action: Read until page nine where the monkeys paint the old car. At that point, give each child a piece of paper in the shape of a car (if you have a die-cutting machine, check to see if you have a car shape). Also give the children markers or crayons and stickers. Unless you have an endless supply of stickers, you may want to limit the number of stickers given to each child. While you read the rest of the story, tell the children to decorate their cars as if they were monkeys trying to sell their cars.

Cousins, Lucy. *Hooray for Fish!*

2005. Cambridge, MA: Candlewick Press.

Summary: Little Fish introduces all sorts of other fish.

Action: Give each child a piece of paper with the outline of a fish and some crayons. Let them color their own fish as you read this book about blue fish, stripy fish, shy fish, and so forth.

DePalma, Mary Newell. *A Grand Old Tree.*

2005. New York: Arthur A. Levine Books.

Summary: A grand old tree provides homes for animals and creates seeds for other trees.

Action: Give each child a piece of paper with the outline of a tree and its branches. Also give them many different-colored leaves cut out of construction paper, a glue stick, and crayons. As you read the story, let the children decorate their trees with leaves and color the trunks and branches.

de Sève, Randall. *Toy Boat.*

2007. Illus., Loren Long. New York: Philomel Books.

Summary: A homemade boat has an adventure at sea, but eventually returns to the boy he loves.

Action: Give each child a piece of paper with the outline of a boat and some crayons. Also give them each a glue stick and a piece of colored tissue paper. As you read the story, the children can color their boats and add tissue paper sails.

Dodd, Emma. *I Love Bugs!*

2010. New York: Holiday House.

Summary: A child describes all the different types of bugs that he likes.

Action: Give each child a piece of paper and some crayons. As you read the story, ask them to draw pictures of their favorite kinds of bugs.

Dunbar, Joyce. *Where's My Sock?*

2006. Illus., Sanja Rescek. New York: Scholastic.

Summary: Pippin and his friend Tog search everywhere for a missing sock.

Action: Give each child a piece of paper with the outline of two socks and some crayons. While you read the story, ask the kids to draw their favorite pair of socks or a pair they would like to have.

Dunbar, Polly. *Dog Blue.*

2004. Cambridge, MA: Candlewick Press.

Summary: Bertie loves the color blue and dreams of owning a blue dog but finds a way to make a black-and-white dog fulfill his wish.

Action: Read the first two pages of this book. After you read "A blue dog!" ask the children what color dog they think would be best. Then give them each a piece of paper with the outline of a dog and some crayons and let them color their favorite color dogs while you finish the story.

Dunbar, Polly. *Flyaway Katie.*

2004. Cambridge, MA: Candlewick Press.

Summary: Katie adds color and fun to her dull life with bright clothing and some paint.

Action: Give each child a piece of paper with the outline of a body and some crayons. As Katie adds color to her life, ask the kids to add color to their pictures. You can have them follow the colors in the book or add their own colorful ideas to Katie's hat, tights (color the legs), shoes, dress, lips, face, arms, and fingers.

Edwards, Pamela Duncan. *Jack and Jill's Treehouse.*
2008. Illus., Henry Cole. New York: Katherine Tegen Books.

> **Summary:** Jack and Jill build and enjoy their tree house in this cumulative tale.
>
> **Action:** Give each child a piece of paper, a glue stick, and six small Popsicle sticks. As you are reading, they can glue the Popsicle sticks into the shape of a wooden house. The simplest design is a square (using four Popsicle sticks) and a triangle on top (using the two remaining Popsicle sticks). Have a premade design on display for the kids to follow.

Emberley, Ed. *Bye-Bye, Big Bad Bullybug!*
2007. New York: Little, Brown.

> **Summary:** A big bullybug appears piece-by-piece on die-cut pages and finally meets his match.
>
> **Action:** Give the children some paper and crayons so they can create their own bullybugs as you read the story. It is recommended that you put a large piece of paper on the flannel board so that you can draw a bullybug for them to follow. Draw the eyes, teeth, mouth, ticklers, pinchers, claws, feet, and belly. The children can follow the colors in the book or use their own imaginations. For added fun, at the end of the story, have everyone put the pictures on the floor and step on them just like the bullybug in the story.

Fox, Mem. *Where Is the Green Sheep?*
2004. Illus., Judy Horacek. Orlando: Harcourt.

> **Summary:** Sheep of all different colors, types, and locations are shown until the green sheep is finally found on the last page.
>
> **Action:** Give each child a piece of paper with the outline of a sheep and a green crayon. Have them color in their sheep as you read the story. On the very last page, have them hold up their green sheep to correspond with the sleeping sheep on that page.

Gliori, Debi. *Flora's Surprise!*

2002. New York: Orchard Books.

> **Summary:** As Flora's family plants a garden, Flora plants a brick and insists that it will be a house one day.

> **Action:** Give each child a piece of paper and some crayons. As you read the story, ask them to draw what they would plant in their gardens.

Gravett, Emily. *The Odd Egg.*

2008. New York: Simon and Schuster Books for Young Readers.

> **Summary:** Duck finds an odd egg that eventually hatches into an alligator.

> **Action:** Give each child a piece of paper in the shape of an egg and some crayons. While you read, let the kids draw spots on their eggs just like the book. When Duck's egg finally starts to crack, the children can rip their eggs in half to simulate the hatching.

Grey, Mini. *Ginger Bear.*

2004. New York: Alfred A. Knopf.

> **Summary:** A gingerbread bear creates friends and then finds a place he will always be safe.

> **Action:** Give each child a piece of paper with the outline of a bear, some crayons, three circles for eyes and a nose, and a glue stick. You can also choose to give them a die-cut bear shape. As you read the story, let the kids add eyes and a nose to their bears and then decorate them using the crayons.

Hall, Michael. *My Heart Is Like a Zoo.*

2010. New York: Greenwillow Books.

> **Summary:** Animals and love are cleverly depicted using hearts.

> **Action:** Give each child some crayons and a piece of paper with the outline of a heart or a piece of paper in the shape of a heart. As you read the book, have them draw their favorite animals inside the hearts.

Harper, Charise Mericle. *Cupcake.*

2010. New York: Disney Hyperion Books.

> **Summary:** A vanilla cupcake is alone after all of his friends are chosen, so he makes friends with a candle.

Action: Give each child a piece of paper with the outline of a cupcake and some crayons. While you read the story, have them create their own fantastic cupcakes. You can also give them glue sticks and cotton balls to include as frosting.

Henkes, Kevin. *Kitten's First Full Moon.*

2004. New York: Greenwillow Books.

Summary: A kitten tries to get to the moon, thinking it is a bowl of milk.

Action: Give each child a paper plate and a few crayons. As you read the story, have the kids each draw a picture of a cat on the plate so Kitten can finally get her milk.

Henkes, Kevin. *Birds.*

2009. Illus., Laura Dronzek. New York: Greenwillow Books.

Summary: Birds of all shapes, sizes, and colors are described.

Action: Give each child a die-cut bird shape, a glue stick, and some feathers. As you read the story, have the kids add feathers to their birds.

Henkes, Kevin. *My Garden.*

2010. New York: Greenwillow Books.

Summary: Flowers change colors, the rabbits are chocolate, and seashells grow in this imaginative garden.

Action: Give each child a blank piece of paper, crayons, a glue stick, a variety of different shapes (circles, rabbits, seashells, jelly beans, birds, butterflies, umbrellas, keys), and some odd buttons. You can pick how many different shapes you supply. While you read the story, let the kids create their own imaginative gardens.

Hoberman, Mary Ann. *Right Outside My Window.*

2002. Illus., Nicholas Wilton. New York: Mondo.

Summary: Birds, clouds, and other scenes are right outside the window during the seasons of the year.

Action: Give each child a piece of paper with the outline of a window and some crayons. As you read the story, have them draw what they see outside one of the windows of their house.

Hubbell, Patricia. *Black All Around!*

2003. Illus., Don Tate. New York: Lee and Low Books.

Summary: A young girl discovers that many things in her life are black (the inside of a pocket, the fuzzy stripes on bumblebees, inky squiggles, etc.).

Action: Give each child a piece of black construction paper and a white crayon. As you read the story, let them draw something that they have seen that is black.

> **alternate book**
>
> You can do this same activity with another book that focuses on the color black: **Black Magic.** Johnson, Dinah. 2010. Illus., R. Gregory Christie. New York: Henry Holt.

Hudson, Cheryl Willis. *Hands Can.*

2003. Illus., John-Francis Bourke. Cambridge, MA: Candlewick Press.

Summary: A celebration of the many things that hands can do.

Action: Give each child a piece of paper and crayon. As you read the story, have them trace their hands on the pieces of paper. At the end of the book, have the children hold up their hand pictures for the whole group to see.

Ichikawa, Satomi. *La La Rose.*

2004. New York: Philomel Books.

Summary: A stuffed rabbit has many adventures in a park while searching for her friend Clementine.

Action: Give each child a paper plate, two pieces of paper in the shape of bunny ears, a glue stick, and some crayons. While you read the story, the kids can glue on the bunny ears and decorate the face of their own La La Rose.

Isadora, Rachel. *Peekaboo Morning.*

2002. New York: G. P. Putnam's Sons.

Summary: A toddler plays peekaboo with family, animals, and toys.

Action: Give each child a piece of paper with a smaller piece of construction paper glued on one side (like a lift-the-flap book) and some crayons. Show them how to fold up the piece of construction paper. While you read the story about playing peekaboo, have them color pictures on the blank pieces of paper so they can play peekaboo with whatever they draw.

Ives, Penny. *Rabbit Pie.*

2006. New York: Viking.

> **Summary:** Mama rabbit cares for her six little ones.
>
> **Action:** Give each child a paper plate and some crayons. As you read the story, ask them to draw some rabbits and carrots on their plates so they can make their own rabbit pies.

Jarrett, Clare. *Arabella Miller's Tiny Caterpillar.*

2008. Cambridge, MA: Candlewick Press.

> **Summary:** Arabella Miller finds a caterpillar and cares for it until it becomes a butterfly.
>
> **Action:** Give each child a bunch of paper circles in a variety of different colors, a glue stick, and some crayons. Ask them each to draw a face on one of the circles, and then glue the circles together in a row to form a caterpillar.

Javernick, Ellen. *The Birthday Pet.*

2009. Illus., Kevin O'Malley. Tarrytown, NY: Marshall Cavendish Children.

> **Summary:** Danny's family gets him lots of different pets before finding the right one for him—a turtle.
>
> **Action:** Give each child a paper plate and some crayons. As you read the story, have them decorate the backs of the paper plates. When the story is finished, give them each a glue stick and five pieces of paper cut to be a turtle's head and legs. They can make their own turtles to bring home with them.

Jenkins, Emily. *Five Creatures.*

2001. Illus., Tomek Bogacki. New York: Frances Foster Books.

> **Summary:** Comparisons of the five creatures that live in this house: three humans and two cats.
>
> **Action:** Give each child a piece of paper with the outline of a house and some crayons. As you read the book, ask them to draw all of the creatures that live in their own houses.

Johnston, Tony. *Cat, What Is That?*

2001. Illus., Wendell Minor. New York: HarperCollins.

> **Summary:** A poetic look at the essence of cats.

Action: As you read the story, have the kids create their own cats. Give each child a paper plate, three paper triangles (to serve as the ears and nose), two paper circles (to serve as the eyes), three pipe cleaners cut in half (to serve as whiskers), a few crayons, and a glue stick. The kids can decorate their plates first with crayons, then glue on the ears, nose, eyes, and whiskers. Make sure the kids remember to draw on a mouth, too.

Kangas, Juli. *The Surprise Visitor.*

2005. New York: Dial Books for Young Readers.

Summary: A mouse finds an egg on his doorstep and tries to find its parents.

Action: Give each child a piece of paper with the outline of an egg and a yellow, blue, and purple crayon. When you get to the part of the story when the turtle paints the egg, ask the kids to color their eggs yellow. When you get to the part of the story when the rabbit adds a face to the egg, ask the kids to draw a blue face on their eggs. Finally, when you get to the part of the story when the squirrel dresses up the egg, ask the kids to draw a purple scarf on their eggs.

Kann, Victoria, and Elizabeth Kann. *Pinkalicious.*

2006. Illus., Victoria Kann. New York: HarperCollins.

Summary: A little girl likes pink so much she turns pink after eating too many pink cupcakes.

Action: Give each child a piece of paper and a pink crayon. Ask them to draw something pink while you read the story.

Kasza, Keiko. *Badger's Fancy Meal.*

2007. New York: G. P. Putnam's Sons.

Summary: Badger unsuccessfully chases a mole, a rat, and a rabbit while looking for something more interesting to eat than what he has in his den.

Action: Give each child a piece of paper and some crayons. While you read the story, have them draw their favorite things to eat.

Kelley, Ellen A. *Buckamoo Girls.*

2006. Illus., Tom Curry. New York: Abrams Books for Young Readers.

Summary: Two cows dream about being cowgirls.

Action: While you read the story, the kids can make cowboy/cowgirl puppets. Give every child a paper lunch bag, a piece of paper in the shape of a cowboy hat, a glue stick, and some crayons. The folded part of the bag is the front; use the fold as the mouth. Have them glue the hats to the very top and then add eyes, a nose, a mouth, and clothes to their puppets.

King, Stephen Michael. *Mutt Dog!*

2004. Orlando: Harcourt.

> **Summary:** A stray dog finds a home with a woman who runs a homeless shelter.
>
> **Action:** Give each child some crayons and a piece of paper that has a small picture of a dog already glued onto it. As you read the story, have the kids draw a home or family for the dog around the dog picture.

Kitamura, Satoshi. *Pablo the Artist.*

2005. New York: Farrar Straus Giroux.

> **Summary:** Pablo the elephant gets help from some friends to make a perfect painting.
>
> **Action:** Put a large sheet of paper up on the wall or flannel board. When Pablo goes to the country and starts to paint, draw a quick tree on the piece of paper. When Pablo falls asleep and a sheep adds something to the painting, ask one child to come up to draw something on your picture. Do the same thing when the squirrel, bird, wild boar, and wolf add to Pablo's painting. If you wish, have every child in the storytime add something to the picture.

Knudson, Michelle. *Library Lion.*

2006. Illus., Kevin Hawkes. Cambridge, MA: Candlewick Press.

> **Summary:** A lion becomes a beloved patron of the local library.
>
> **Action:** Give each child a paper plate, a glue stick, some crayons, and yarn scraps. As you read the story, the kids can glue yarn around the outside of the plates like a lion's mane and can draw the lion's face with the crayons.

Krosoczka, Jarrett J. *Baghead.*

2002. New York: Alfred A. Knopf.

> **Summary:** Josh wears a bag over his head all day in order to hide a bad haircut.

Action: Give each child some crayons and a large grocery bag with a hole cut out for their face. As you read, they can decorate their bags so they can be bagheads, too.

Krosoczka, Jarrett J. *Bubble Bath Pirates!*

2003. New York: Viking.

> **Summary:** A mother gives her two pirate boys a bath.
>
> **Action:** Give each child a paper eye patch and some crayons. (Punch two small holes in the eye patches before handing them out.) They can design their own pirate eye patches while you read the story. At the end of storytime, have string available and ask the other adults in the room to help you tie the eye patches on each child.

Landry, Leo. *Eat Your Peas, Ivy Louise!*

2005. Boston: Houghton Mifflin.

> **Summary:** Instead of eating her peas, Ivy Louise watches them perform in a circus.
>
> **Action:** Give each child a green construction paper circle and some crayons. While you read the story, they can create their own pea masterpieces.

Lerner, Harriet, and Susan Goldhor. *Franny B. Kranny, There's a Bird in Your Hair!*

2001. Illus., Helen Oxenbury. New York: HarperCollins.

> **Summary:** Franny has wild and frizzy hair that she refuses to cut, until a bird makes a nest in her hair and advises her to cut it.
>
> **Action:** Give each child a paper plate, some crayons, a glue stick, and some yarn scraps. As you read the story, they can create their own versions of Franny with wild, unruly hair made out of yarn.

Lucas, David. *Halibut Jackson.*

2003. New York: Alfred A. Knopf.

> **Summary:** Halibut Jackson likes to wear clothing that helps him fit in and becomes the star of the party at the Palace.
>
> **Action:** After receiving the invitation to the Palace, Halibut Jackson creates a silver and gold suit so he can blend in. At that point in the story, give

every child a picture of a person and a silver and gold crayon. Have them each create a suit for Halibut to wear to the party.

Lucas, David. *Something to Do.*

2008. New York: Philomel Books.

> **Summary:** Little Bear and Big Bear create their own fun by drawing in the sand.
>
> **Action:** Give every child a piece of paper and a crayon. Have them draw along with the bears. They can create a line, a ladder, a moon, and stars.

Lyon, George Ella. *Weaving the Rainbow.*

2004. Illus., Stephanie Anderson. New York: A Richard Jackson Book.

> **Summary:** A weaver raises sheep, shears their wool, and creates a beautiful picture from the yarn.
>
> **Action:** Give each child a piece of paper with the outline of a sheep, a glue stick, and some cotton balls. As you read the story, they can create their own fluffy sheep like the ones in the book. You can also substitute a die-cut sheep shape for the outline of the sheep.

McCarty, Peter. *Jeremy Draws a Monster.*

2009. New York: Henry Holt.

> **Summary:** Jeremy draws a very needy monster that demands a sandwich, a chair, a telephone, and so on.
>
> **Action:** Give each child a blank piece of paper and some crayons. While you read the story, ask them to draw their own monsters. If you have a toy bus, have the children put their monster drawings inside the bus at the end of the story (just like Jeremy's monster).

McDonald, Megan. *It's Picture Day Today!*

2009. Illus., Katherine Tillotson. New York: Atheneum Books for Young Readers.

> **Summary:** Different objects and art supplies come together for picture day at school.
>
> **Action:** Give each child a blank piece of paper, a glue stick, and a variety of objects from the story: buttons, feathers, string, pom-poms, and ribbon. While you read the story, they can create their own picture day images. If you want to follow the storyline more closely, you can wait to give out glue sticks until the missing glue is found.

McDonnell, Patrick. *Art.*

2006. New York: Little, Brown.

Summary: Art draws art of all types and colors.

Action: Give each child a blank piece of paper and some crayons. Have them color along with Art: draw zigzags, scribbles that squiggle, dots, splotches, and curly cues. Since Art's mom hangs his art on the refrigerator, tell the kids to ask their parents to hang their art somewhere when they get home.

Meade, Holly. *A Place to Sleep.*

2001. New York: Marshall Cavendish.

Summary: Tired animals show where they sleep.

Action: At the very end of the book, readers are asked where two children sleep. At that point, give everyone a piece of paper with the outline of a bed, a glue stick, and a piece of colored tissue. While you finish the last couple of pages, they can glue the tissue onto the bed like a blanket.

Menchin, Scott. *Taking a Bath with the Dog and Other Things That Make Me Happy.*

2007. Cambridge, MA: Candlewick Press.

Summary: When Sweet Pea isn't happy, she asks others what makes them happy to find her own smile.

Action: Sweet Pea asks lots of people and objects what makes them happy. Give every child a blank piece of paper and some crayons. While you read the story, ask them to draw something that makes them happy.

Milton, Giles. *Call Me Gorgeous!*

2009. Illus., Alexandra Milton. New York: Boxer Books.

Summary: An odd animal is described by its many conflicting parts.

Action: Give every child a blank piece of paper and some crayons. Put a large piece of paper on your flannel board so you can follow along with the activity as well. As you read each page, both you and the children can start drawing the animal that is described: reindeer antlers, pig ears, porcupine spines, crocodile teeth, toucan beak, flamingo neck, rooster feet, Dalmatian spots, chameleon tail, bat wings, and frog eyes. At the end of the book, compare your animals to the one in the story.

Moulton, Mark Kimball. *The Very Best Pumpkin.*

2010. Illus., Karen Hillard Good. New York: A Paula Wiseman Book.

> **Summary:** Peter dutifully cares for a special pumpkin on the farm. This pumpkin ends up being the perfect one for Meg and her family.
>
> **Action:** Give every child a die-cut orange pumpkin shape and some crayons. Since pumpkins are often used to make jack-o-lanterns, have the children create their own special designs while you read the story.

Muldrow, Diane. *We Planted a Tree.*

2010. Illus., Bob Staake. New York: A Golden Book.

> **Summary:** A tree is planted; as it grows it helps heal the world.
>
> **Action:** Give each child a piece of paper with the outline of a tree and some crayons. As you read the story, they can decorate their own special trees.

Murphy, Yannick. *Baby Polar.*

2009. Illus., Kristen Balouch. New York: Clarion Books.

> **Summary:** Baby Polar plays in the snow, has trouble finding his mother when the snow gets deep, and finally hears her heart beat and is able to get warm again.
>
> **Action:** Give everyone a red heart cut out of paper, a glue stick, and some cotton balls. Have the kids glue the cotton onto one side of their hearts so that they have a mama polar bear heart to keep them warm.

Na, Il Sung. *A Book of Sleep.*

2007. New York: Alfred A. Knopf.

> **Summary:** Many animals sleep at night, except for owl, who is wide awake.
>
> **Action:** Give every child a paper plate, two large paper circles, a slightly smaller paper triangle, a glue stick, and some crayons. While you read the story about the animals that are sleeping, the kids can create their own owls to stay up during the night. Have them use the paper circles and triangle as the eyes and nose, and the crayons to create a mouth and feathers.

Neubecker, Robert. *Courage of the Blue Boy.*

2006. Berkeley, CA: Tricycle Press.

> **Summary:** Blue and his friend, Polly, leave a world filled with only blue things in search of other colors.

Action: Give everyone a piece of blank paper and a blue crayon. While you read the story, have them draw something in their world that is blue.

Newton, Jill. *Bored! Bored! Bored!*

2002. New York: Bloomsbury Children's Books.

Summary: Claude the shark discovers that baking is less boring than gardening.

Action: Give each child a piece of blue paper and some crayons. While you read the story, have them create their own underwater gardens.

Niemann, Christoph. *The Police Cloud.*

2007. New York: Schwartz and Wade Books.

Summary: A cloud wants to be a police officer but is poorly made for the job.

Action: Give each child a piece of paper with the outline of a cloud or a die-cut cloud shape, a glue stick, and some cotton balls. While you read the story, they can create their own clouds. At the end of the story, the cloud realizes that he makes a better member of the fire department than the police department. Give everyone a red paper fire hat to add to their clouds.

Park, Linda Sue. *What Does Bunny See?*

2005. Illus., Maggie Smith. New York: Clarion Books.

Summary: A rabbit wanders through a garden and sees flowers of various colors.

Action: Give each child a blank piece of paper and seven crayons: red, yellow, purple, green, pink, orange, and blue. When the bunny finds the red poppies, have the children hold up their red crayons and then draw a red flower on their papers. Continue with each of the plants that the bunny finds: yellow primroses, purple violets, green grass, pink water lilies, orange tiger lilies, and blue morning glories.

Pedersen, Janet. *Millie in the Meadow.*

2003. Cambridge, MA: Candlewick Press.

Summary: A cow watches an artist draw her friends and hopes he will add her to the picture.

Action: Give each child a blank piece of paper and some crayons. Have them draw along with the artist: a ladybug, a spider, a rabbit, and finally, a cow.

Portis, Antoinette. *A Penguin Story.*

2009. New York: HarperCollins.

> **Summary:** A penguin goes off in search of something that isn't white, black, or blue and finds a camp of humans with lots of orange things.
>
> **Action:** Give each child a piece of blank white paper, a black crayon, and a blue crayon. While you read the first part of the story, everyone can draw things that are black or blue. When you get to the part of the story when the penguin finds the camp, give everyone an orange crayon. While you finish the story, everyone can draw things that are black, blue, or orange.

Proimos, James. *Patricia von Pleasantsquirrel.*

2009. New York: Dial Books for Young Readers.

> **Summary:** Patricia sets off to find a place where she can be a princess, but she discovers that being a princess can be hard work.
>
> **Action:** Give every child a paper crown and some crayons and/or stickers. Paper crowns can be found at most party supply stores. While you read the story, the children can decorate their crowns so that they can be princesses or princes when they go home.

Rickards, Lynne. *Pink!*

2009. Illus., Margaret Chamberlain. New York: Chicken House.

> **Summary:** When Patrick the penguin wakes up pink, he leaves his penguin family to try to find a place where he will belong.
>
> **Action:** Give everyone a piece of paper with the outline of a penguin and some crayons. While you read the story, the children can color their penguins using unique colors. At the end of the story, have them hold up their penguins to show how wonderfully different they all are.

Rohmann, Eric. *Clara and Asha.*

2005. New Milford, CT: Roaring Brook Press.

> **Summary:** Clara and her imaginary giant fish, Asha, play before bedtime.
>
> **Action:** Give every child a piece of paper with the outline of a fish, a glue stick, and some pieces of paper in the shape of fish scales. You can also use a die-cut fish shape for this activity. While you read the story, the kids can glue scales on their paper fish so that they have their own versions of Asha to play with before bedtime.

Rohmann, Eric. *A Kitten Tale.*

2008. New York: Alfred A. Knopf.

Summary: Three kittens worry about snow while a fourth one can't wait.

Action: Give everyone a piece of paper with the outline of a cat (or a die-cut cat), a glue stick, and some cotton balls. While you read the story, the kids can glue the cotton "snow" onto their kittens.

Rumford, James. *Calabash Cat and His Amazing Journey.*

2003. Boston: Houghton Mifflin.

Summary: Calabash Cat gets help from many animals on his quest to find the end of the world.

Action: Give everyone a blank piece of paper and a red, orange, yellow, green, blue, and purple crayon. Whenever Calabash Cat enters another part of the world and travels with another animal, his journey is illustrated with a new color line. When Calabash Cat is traveling on the red line, the kids can draw a red line on their pieces of paper. Have them continue to make their lines longer and longer using the different colors as they appear in the story.

Rylant, Cynthia. *Long Night Moon.*

2004. Illus., Mark Siegel. New York: Simon and Schuster Books for Young Readers.

Summary: Each month, the moon changes and has a new personality.

Action: Give each child a paper plate and some crayons. While you read about the different moons throughout the year, they can draw pictures of the man on the moon on their paper plate moons.

Sattler, Jennifer. *Sylvie.*

2009. New York: Random House.

Summary: Sylvie the flamingo discovers that eating things that aren't pink will make her turn different colors.

Action: Give each child a piece of paper with the outline of a flamingo and some crayons. As Sylvie turns different colors in the story, the kids can follow along with the same color or design.

Schaefer, Lola M. *This Is the Sunflower.*

2000. Illus., Donald Crews. New York: Greenwillow Books.

> **Summary:** A cumulative tale about a sunflower that grows and creates seeds for more sunflowers.
>
> **Action:** Give each child a paper plate, a glue stick, some yellow paper petals, a black crayon, and a brown crayon. As you read the story, they can color the sunflower seeds on their plates and glue the petals on to make their own sunflowers.

Schoonmaker, Elizabeth. *Square Cat.*

2011. New York: Aladdin.

> **Summary:** Eula the square cat learns that it's okay to be different.
>
> **Action:** Give everyone a square piece of construction paper, two small construction paper triangles (cat ears), a piece of string (cat tail), a glue stick, and some crayons. While you read the story, the kids can make their own square cats to bring home with them.

Stevenson, Robert Louis. *The Moon.*

2006. Illus., Tracey Campbell Pearson. New York: Farrar Straus Giroux.

> **Summary:** An illustrated version of Stevenson's poem about the moon.
>
> **Action:** The very first line of the poem reads: "The moon has a face like the clock in the hall." Give every child a paper plate and some crayons. While you read the story, they can draw faces on their own paper plate moons.

Stojic, Manya. *Rain.*

2000. New York: Crown Publishers.

> **Summary:** The animals enjoy the rain that finally comes to the hot African savanna.
>
> **Action:** Before starting the story, give everyone a plain piece of paper. Show them how to make a fan by folding the paper back and forth accordion style. Then pinch one end together and flap the wide end near your face like a fan. Use the fan at the very beginning and the very end of the book when everything and everyone is hot. When the rain starts, have the children put their fans down and make rain with their fingers. They can hold their arms out in front of their bodies and wiggle their fingers to imitate rain. You can make this into a longer art activity by having

the children decorate their pieces of paper with crayons before folding them into fans.

Swope, Sam. *Gotta Go! Gotta Go!*

2000. Illus., Sue Riddle. New York: Farrar, Straus and Giroux.

Summary: A Monarch butterfly caterpillar transforms into a butterfly and makes the long trip to Mexico.

Action: When the caterpillar changes into a butterfly, give everyone a piece of paper with the outline of a butterfly and some crayons. While you finish reading the story, the children can create their own beautiful butterflies.

Thomson, Bill. *Chalk.*

2010. Tarrytown, NY: Marshall Cavendish Children.

Summary: Three children draw with chalk and their drawings come to life.

Action: If you have enough little chalkboards for everyone in your program, give everyone a chalkboard and a piece of chalk. If you don't have chalkboards, a piece of paper and a crayon will also work. Have the children draw along with the kids in this book. They can draw the sun, a butterfly, and a dinosaur. Finally, have them draw a rain cloud so that the imaginary dinosaur goes away.

Tseng, Kevin. *Ned's New Home.*

2009. Berkeley, CA: Tricycle Press.

Summary: Ned the worm has to move out of his apple and struggles to find another fruit to live in.

Action: Give every child a piece of paper with the outline of an apple and some crayons. While you read the story, they can draw the perfect home for the worm inside of their apples.

Tusa, Tricia. *Follow Me.*

2001. Boston: Houghton Mifflin Harcourt.

Summary: A girl travels through an imaginative world of colors.

Action: Give every child a blank piece of paper and the following crayons: pink, blue, purple, gray, green, brown, yellow, orange, and red. As the young girl travels through each color, have everyone draw with each particular color. The kids can draw whatever they want.

Vrombaut, An. *Clarabella's Teeth.*

2003. New York: Clarion Books.

> **Summary:** Clarabella the crocodile has so many teeth that it takes her all day to brush them.
>
> **Action:** Make a crocodile puppet with lots of teeth to bring home. Give every child a paper bag, some crayons, a glue stick, and a bunch of triangles cut out of white paper. The fold in the paper bag can be the crocodile's mouth. While you read the story, the kids can color their crocodiles and glue lots of teeth inside their mouths.

Walker, Rob D. *Once Upon a Cloud.*

2005. Illus., Matt Mahurin. New York: The Blue Sky Press.

> **Summary:** Children wonder about clouds and what they really are.
>
> **Action:** Give each child a handful of cotton balls and a glue stick. While you read the story, they can create their own clouds to bring home with them. If this activity is too difficult, you can give them each a piece of paper to glue the cotton balls to in order to make a cloud.

Ward, Jennifer. *The Busy Tree.*

2009. Illus., Lisa Falkenstern. Tarrytown, NY: Marshall Cavendish Children.

> **Summary:** A busy tree reveals all of the wildlife living in its branches.
>
> **Action:** Give the children a piece of paper with the outline of a tree and some crayons. While you read the story, they can draw animals and leaves on their trees.

Warnes, Tim. *Mommy Mine.*

2005. Illus., Jane Chapman. New York: HarperCollins.

———. *Daddy Hug.*

2008. Illus., Jane Chapman. New York: HarperCollins.

> **Summary:** Animals show how there are many different types of mommies and daddies.
>
> **Action:** Give each child a blank piece of paper and some crayons. As you read the story, have them draw pictures of their mommies or daddies. These books/activities are great around Mother's Day and Father's Day.

Weeks, Sarah. *I'm a Pig.*

2005. Illus., Holly Berry. New York: Laura Geringer Books.

Summary: A pig tells the reader all the reasons it is great to be a pig.

Action: Give each child a paper plate and some crayons. If you can find pink paper plates, that is even better. While you read the story, the kids can draw pig faces on their paper plates. At the end of the story, give everyone a short piece of yarn and a piece of tape to add to the back of the paper plates like a pig tail.

Wellington, Monica. *Pizza at Sally's.*

2006. New York: Dutton Children's Books.

Summary: Sally gets everything she needs to make a great pizza for her shop.

Action: Give every child a paper plate and some crayons. While you read the story, they can draw their favorite kind of pizza.

Wild, Margaret. *Piglet and Papa.*

2007. Illus., Stephen Michael King. New York: Abrams Books for Young Readers.

Summary: When Piglet upsets her father, she goes in search of someone else who loves her and discovers that Papa still loves her the most.

Action: Give every child a piece of paper with the outline of a heart and some crayons. While you read the story, have the children draw pictures of someone who loves them or someone they love.

Willis, Jeanne. *Cottonball Colin.*

2007. Illus., Tony Ross. Grand Rapids, MI: Eerdmans Books for Young Readers.

Summary: Colin the mouse is so small that his mother wraps him in cotton to try to protect him.

Action: When you get to the part of the story where Colin's mother wraps him up in cotton, give everyone a die-cut mouse shape, some cotton balls, and a glue stick. While you finish the story, the children can create their own versions of cotton-wrapped Colin to bring home with them.

Wilson, Karma. *Princess Me.*

2007. Illus., Christa Unzner. New York: Margaret K. McElderry Books.

Summary: A young girl pretends to be a sweet and kind princess.

Action: Give every child a paper crown and some crayons. (Paper crowns can be found at most party supply stores.) While you read the story, the children can decorate their crowns so that they can be princes or princesses, too. If you wish, give them other items to decorate their crowns such as stickers, cotton balls, feathers, and so forth.

———. *Where Is Home, Little Pip?*
2008. Illus., Jane Chapman. New York: Margaret K. McElderry Books.
   Summary: When a little penguin wanders far from home, she asks other animals for help.
   Action: Give every child a blank piece of paper and some crayons. While you read the story, they can draw pictures of their homes.

Wilson-Max, Ken. *Max Paints the House.*
2000. New York: Hyperion Books for Children.
   Summary: Max, Little Pig, and Big Blue try to paint their house to match the sky.
   Action: Give everyone a piece of paper with the outline of a house and the following crayons: red, pink, orange, yellow, green, blue, and purple. If possible, give them two different colors of purple so that you have all of the colors of the rainbow (plus pink). As Max and his friends paint their house different colors, have the kids use their crayons to add the same colors to their house pictures. When Max and his friends paint their house like a rainbow, the kids can draw rainbows over their house pictures.

Wright, Michael. *Jake Stays Awake.*
2007. New York: Feiwel and Friends.
   Summary: Jake's parents try to get Jake to sleep somewhere besides in their bed with them.
   Action: Give everyone a piece of paper with the outline of a bed, some crayons, a glue stick, and a piece of construction paper just large enough to be a blanket for the bed. While you read the story, each of the kids can create a bed that Jake will want to sleep in.

Ziefert, Harriet. *One Red Apple.*

2009. Illus., Karla Gudeon. Maplewood, NJ: Blue Apple Books.

Summary: An apple grows from seed, to tree, to fruit, and then repeats.

Action: Give everyone a piece of paper with the outline of an apple and a red crayon. While you read the story, the kids can color their own red apples.

games

Hide-and-seek and follow the leader! The characters get to play games in their stories and this is the chance for your program attendees to play along. Take a quick break from the story to search for a missing mitten in your storytime space. Or create movement patterns to mimic patterns in the book. Simple instructions are provided for each game. Who is the best copycat in your storytime? Everyone is a winner when you have this much fun during storytime.

tips

- Ask adults in the room to help by playing the games with their children.
- Keep rules simple. For example, when kids are looking for an object in a storytime space, use the following rules: Everyone please look for the (object). If you find the object please bring it to me. When you hear me blow the whistle, please return to your seats. (Blow the whistle when the object has been found.)
- Help the children learn to take turns. If you are asking one child to come up and help, you may want to walk into the group and take that child

by the hand to lead them to the front of the room. Pointing to a child raising his or her hand may lead to confusion.

- Use a bell or other noisemaker to signal when it is time to settle down for more of the book. For example, when reading *Whose Nose and Toes?* you can ring a bell to signal when it is time to stop acting like a particular animal. Be sure to practice this a few times before you start reading the book. You can practice by having the kids jump in place and asking them to stop as soon as they hear the bell.
- Practice some of the activities with the children before you read the book. If you are going to ask them to imitate your movements during a story such as *Orange Pear Apple Bear,* practice a few sequences before you start reading the book. Demonstrate the appropriate actions for musical activities as well. Practice how to stop moving whenever the music stops.
- Put tape on the floor before a program starts if you are going to ask the children to sit in a circle. Then ask the kids to stand on the tape to form a circle. You can also use a round or oval rug and ask the kids to stand on the edge.

tip How you do this will depend on your library space. If you have a separate storytime room, you can fill the room with many different objects that the kids have to sort through to find Tilly's objects. This will be a little more difficult on the library floor. If possible, set up a barrier with chairs, or ask parents to act as barriers around a large area with the objects.

Ahlberg, Allan. *Treasure Hunt.*

2002. Illus., Gillian Tyler. Cambridge, MA: Candlewick Press.

Summary: Tilly goes on many scavenger hunts throughout her day.

Action: Set up a scavenger hunt so the children can find the same objects as Tilly: a banana, a stuffed rabbit, a stuffed cat, and gold-wrapped coins. When Tilly's parents hide themselves, let the kids "find" their parents or caregiver. Let the kids search for each item as it comes up in the story and then keep reading until the next object.

Alakija, Polly. *Catch That Goat!*

2002. Cambridge, MA: Barefoot Books.

Summary: Ayoka loses track of her goat in a Nigerian street market.

Action: Spread pictures of all of the items in the book throughout the story-time space. When you get to each page, have the children locate the items. For example, have them find ten pictures of boli. After the ten pictures have been found, count them together and then go on to the next page of the book. You can photocopy images from the book or find generic images by doing a search on the Internet. It is recommended that you laminate the pictures so that they will last for future storytimes.

Barrett, Judi. *Which Witch is Which?*

2001. Illus., Sharleen Collicott. New York: Atheneum Books for Young Readers.
Summary: Study the accompanying picture to solve each riddle.
Action: Solve the riddles on each page by studying the illustrations with the kids. Note that this particular activity is probably best with a small, older preschool group.

Beaton, Clare. *Daisy Gets Dressed.*

2005. Cambridge, MA: Barefoot Books.
Summary: Daisy gets dressed wearing a variety of patterns.
Action: Have a piece of fabric to represent each of the patterns listed in the book: zigzag, checkered, striped, wavy, flowery, starry, spotted, spiral, and diamond. As you put each piece of fabric on your flannel board, ask the kids to describe it and give them the right descriptive word. As you read the story, have different children come up and identify the same pattern fabric on your flannel board.

Blackstone, Stella. *Jump into January.*

2004. Illus., Maria Carluccio. Cambridge, MA: Barefoot Books.
Summary: Find things on every page related to the months of the year.
Action: Play the seek-and-find on each page of this book. Depending on the size and age of the group, you may want to pick only a couple of easy-to-find objects on each page. Or, you may want to do only one page a week until the book is complete.

Blackstone, Stella. *Secret Seahorse.*

2004. Illus., Clare Beaton. Cambridge, MA: Barefoot Books.
Summary: Explore a coral reef as you try to find a seahorse.

alternate activity

You can also hide seahorse images (or stuffed seahorses) in your storytime space. Pause on one of the pages to have everyone search for the seahorses in storytime or do the search at the end of the book.

Action: The seahorse is on almost every page on this book. Call up one child for each page to help you find the seahorse in that illustration.

Bloom, Suzanne. *The Bus for Us.*

2001. Honesdale, PA: Boyds Mills Press.

Summary: As Tess waits for her first trip on a school bus, she learns about other vehicles.

Action: Readers see a small portion of each vehicle as it approaches the bus stop and kids can guess what each vehicle is before the page is turned. This book is very short so you can also have the kids stand throughout the book and move around the room like each vehicle as it becomes fully present.

Butler, John. *Whose Nose and Toes?*

2004. New York: Viking.

Summary: Each page has the nose and toes of a baby animal for kids to identify before turning the page.

Action: After you read "Whose nose and toes?" on each page, have the kids guess the animal then act like that animal:

- For the baby tiger, crawl around and roar.
- For the baby pig, crawl around and oink.
- For the duckling, waddle and quack.
- For the rhino, snort.
- For the giraffe, stretch your neck up tall.
- For the puppy, play and bark.
- For the monkey, pretend to swing through the trees.
- For the calf, crawl and moo.
- For the crocodile, make a big mouth with your arms and snap them together.
- For the elephant, pretend to spray water on yourself using your arm as a trunk.

Coffelt, Nancy. *Big, Bigger, Biggest!*

2009. New York: Henry Holt.

Summary: Animals compare who is biggest, smallest, fastest, slowest, hungriest, slimiest, and sleepiest.

Action: Try to act out the different traits of the animals and have the kids follow along:

- For the big hippopotamus, stand tall and try to make yourself big; for the bigger killer whale, try to make yourself even bigger; for the biggest dinosaur, try to make yourself even bigger.
- For the smallest animals, shrink down to the floor to make yourself small.
- For the fastest animals, run in place.
- For the slowest animals, move very slowly.
- For the hungriest animals, rub your stomach.
- For the slimiest animals, rub your arm and make a face as if your arm is sticky and slimy.
- Finally, for the sleepiest animals, start by laying your head on your hands, then sit down, and then lie down.
- Make a game out of this book by seeing who can be biggest, smallest, fastest, and slowest.

Dillon, Leo, and Diane Dillon. *Rap a Tap Tap: Here's Bojangles— Think of That!*

2002. New York: The Blue Sky Press.

Summary: An illustrated interpretation of a legendary dancer's life.

Action: The words "Rap a tap tap—think of that!" appear thirteen times in the text. Every time they appear, do a different clapping, slapping, stomping, and so forth, sequence and have the kids repeat the rhythm. For example, as you read the phrase the first time, clap your hands three times: RAP a TAP TAP. The second time, stomp your feet three times. The third time, clap, stomp, clap. See who can play this imitation game the best.

Gravett, Emily. *Orange Pear Apple Bear.*

2005. New York: Simon and Schuster Books for Young Readers.

Summary: An exploration of colors and foods using only five words.

Action: Create a movement for the four main words in this book. For example: Orange—clap, Pear—stomp, Apple—turn around, Bear—jump. See who can remember the motions best as you read the story. The four words appear in multiple sequences throughout the book.

Harris, Trudy. *Pattern Fish.*

2000. Illus., Anne Canevari Green. Brookfield, CT: The Millbrook Press.

Summary: Underwater animals are described through patterns.

Action: Continue the use of patterns in this book by creating corresponding movement patterns for each animal. All of the patterns are repeated at the end; see who can remember which movements go with which patterns. Some potential patterns are:

- yellow-black—clap-stomp
- stripe-dot-dot—clap-jump-jump
- chomp-chomp-munch-munch—clap-clap-bend knees-bend knees
- bubble-bubble-pop—clap-clap-arms in the air
- stretch-spurt-glide—stretch neck-clap-jump
- wiggle-jiggle-jiggle-float—shake body-clap-clap-stomp
- splash-turn-swish-dive—clap-turn around-stomp-jump

Helldorfer, M. C. *Got to Dance.*

2004. Illus., Hiroe Nakata. New York: A Doubleday Book for Young Readers.

Summary: A little girl dances through her day with Grandpa.

Action: Play a few seconds of music at the end of each page. Create a different dance/movement for each page and have the kids play follow the leader. Some of the pages lend themselves to a specific dance/movement:

- Pretend to hold a pan and flip pancakes for the "pancakes are flipping" page.
- Hop back and forth quickly for "the burning hot street" page.
- Stand tall and waddle for the "penguin dance" page.
- Flap your arms like a bird for the "every-birdy dance" page.
- Hop on one foot for the "hoppity-hop dance" page.

- Jump up and down for the "boing-boing dance" page.
- Bend at your waist for the "upside-down dance" page.
- Pretend to tap dance for the "tap dancing tap tap" page.
- For the other pages, dance/move however you wish.

Ho, Minfong. *Peek! A Thai Hide-and-Seek.*

2004. Illus., Holly Meade. Cambridge, MA: Candlewick Press.

Summary: A father finds many animals while he searches for his daughter so they can play Jut-Ay (peekaboo).

Action: The words "Jut-Ay" appear twelve times in this book. Play peekaboo with the kids every time you read those words. Play the game using your hands or juggling scarves.

Horáček, Petr. *My Elephant.*

2009. Somerville, MA: Candlewick Press.

Summary: A boy and his imaginary elephant get into trouble together at Grandpa and Grandma's house.

Action: Split the group into two teams. Have each team sit in a semicircle. Show the kids the book and ask them what food elephants like to eat. When someone guesses peanuts, give each team one peanut (you may need to use a fake peanut because of nut allergies). The object is to pass the peanut quickly around the semicircle to see which team finishes first. It may be best to do this after reading the book in its entirety, or take a break from reading after the elephant is introduced to the story. If you need to make the game more difficult, give each child a sock to wear on his or her hand as an elephant trunk.

Jocelyn, Marthe. *Same Same.*

2009. Illus., Tom Slaughter. Toronto: Tundra Books.

Summary: Different sets of objects are illustrated.

Action: Find a variety of different objects that you can set around your storytime space. The objects can be pictures, toys, trinkets, and so forth. Make sure many of them match at least one set in the book: round things, things that make music, things that fly, striped things, long things, things that go, things in water, very big things, things with four legs, and red things. The objects you set around the room can fit more than one set. After you show and read each set in the book, ask the kids to walk around to find something else that fits that same set. Ask a few kids to show what they found. After finishing that set, bring all of the objects back to the front of the room. Now continue with the other sets doing the same activity.

Kellogg, Steven. *The Missing Mitten Mystery.*

2000. New York: Dial Books for Young Readers.

Summary: Annie loses her mitten in the snow and discovers it has become part of a snowman.

Action: Hide numerous mittens around the storytime area. After reading the first page of the story, have the kids search the area for the missing mittens. As they find a mitten, they should have a seat to get ready for the rest of the story. Once all of the mittens have been found, finish the story to see where Annie's lost mitten ended up.

Kwan, Yoon-duck. *My Cat Copies Me.*

2007. La Jolla, CA: Kane/Miller Book.

Summary: A girl and her cat bond while copying each other throughout the day.

Action: Since the girl and the cat copy each other, play a follow the leader game after you read each page. You can try to find actions that fit the page you just read or do a simple clapping and stomping rhythm for the kids to follow.

Lee, Spike, and Tonya Lewis. *Please, Puppy, Please.*

2005. Illus., Kadir Nelson. New York: Simon and Schuster Books for Young Readers.

Summary: A boy and girl spend a day with their rambunctious puppy.

Action: A combination of the words *puppy* and *please* appear on each page of the book. Teach the kids to clap every time you read the word *puppy* and stomp every time you read the word *please*. Since the combination and order of the words change on each page, see who can get it right each time.

Liu, Jae Soo. *Yellow Umbrella.*

2002. La Jolla, CA: Kane/Miller Book.

Summary: Different-colored umbrellas join each consecutive page.

Action: Give each child a piece of paper and a crayon for each color umbrella in the book. On the first page, have them draw a yellow circle on their paper to represent the yellow umbrella. On the second page, a blue umbrella shows up. Ask the kids to figure out what color is new. Once someone figures out it is the blue umbrella, have them draw a blue circle on their paper. A new umbrella joins the story on each page and the game gets harder and harder. You may want to have a cheat sheet for yourself for the last few pages.

Marino, Gianna. *One Too Many: A Seek and Find Counting Book.*

2010. San Francisco: Chronicle Books.

Summary: A barnyard trough is overrun with more and more animals.

Action: On the first page, there is one flea. On the second page, there is one flea and two cows. On the third page, there is one flea, two cows, and three horses. On each page it gets harder and harder to determine which animal is new. Play a game by asking the kids to study the pages and act like the new animal that they see. They can make the noise of the new animal or make movements like the new animal. Who can find the new animal first? The last page has a key for you to follow if the game gets too difficult.

> **tip** If the game is too hard, create a felt piece for each type of animal in the book: flea, cow, horse, goat, sheep, pig, bunny, goose, chicken, mouse, firefly, bat, and skunk. After the kids find the new animal on the page, add that felt piece to your flannel board as a reminder of the "old" animals.

O'Hair, Margaret. *My Pup.*

2008. Illus., Tammie Lyon. Tarrytown, NY: Marshall Cavendish Children.

Summary: A little girl and her new puppy have lots of fun together throughout the day.

Action: The word *puppy* appears 42 times in the text. Give everyone a bell or shaker to play every time you read the word *puppy*. See who can keep up.

Olson, Mary W. *Nice Try, Tooth Fairy.*

2000. Illus., Katherine Tillotson. New York: Simon and Schuster Books for Young Readers.

Summary: Emma asks the tooth fairy to return her lost tooth so she can show her grandfather, but the tooth fairy keeps bringing the wrong tooth.

Action: Before the program, cut a tooth shape out of white paper. Hide the tooth somewhere in your storytime space. When you get to the page in the book where the tooth fairy is looking through her files, ask everyone to search the storytime space for Emma's tooth. Continue with the story once the tooth is found.

Park, Linda Sue. *Mung-Mung: A Fold-Out Book of Animal Sounds.*

2004. Illus., Diane Bigda. Watertown, MA: Charlesbridge.

Summary: A guessing game of animals based on the sounds they make in different languages.

Action: Eight different animals are shown in this book. For each animal, the sounds that they make are written in five different languages. The kids can guess the animals as you read the different sounds. When they think they know what animal it is, they should start to act like that animal and use the English version of their sound. For example, the first animal says: "Mung-mung" in Korean, "Bo-bo" in Hindi, "Gav-gav" in Russian, "Wow-wow" in Spanish, and finally "Woof-woof" in English. If the children think you are talking about a dog, they should bark and make movements that they think are doglike. Each page lists the English version of the animal sound; be sure to read that sound last as you lift the flap to reveal the animal.

Payne, Nina. *Four in All.*

2001. Illus., Adam Payne. Asheville, NC: Front Street.

Summary: A young girl's adventure is told in a poem that uses only four words per page.

Action: Since only four words are used on each page, create a movement for each word. For example, clap on the first word, stomp on the second word, turn around on the third word, and jump on the fourth word. Use this same sequence on every page. Since the words change on each page, see who can remember how to do the correct action sequence as you read the book. You can make the game easier by doing the actions with the kids.

Provencher, Rose-Marie. *Slithery Jake.*

2004. Illus., Abby Carter. New York: HarperCollins.

Summary: Sid brings home a pet snake, but it goes missing in the middle of the night.

Action: Hide a stuffed snake or snake picture in your storytime area before the program begins. When you reach the part of the story where the whole family is looking for Jake the Snake, pause reading so everyone in storytime can search for him, too. Once your snake is found, continue reading to see where Jake was hidden.

Ruelle, Karen Gray. *Bark Park.*

2008. Atlanta: Peachtree.

Summary: Dogs of all shapes and sizes play in the park.

Action: Every time you read the word *dog*, everyone should jump up and bark. The word *dog* appears 31 times in the text (once as the word *doggie*). Who will hear all of them?

Smee, Nicola. *What's the Matter, Bunny Blue?*

2010. New York: Boxer Books.

Summary: When Bunny Blue can't find her grandmother, a bee, duck, tiger, crocodile, bear, and fox help her find Granny.

Action: Before the program starts, hide a blue bunny (stuffed bunny or blue paper bunny) somewhere in your storytime space. As you read the story, Bunny says "Boo Hoo Hoo!" many times in response to the questions asked by the other animals. Whenever Bunny cries like that, hold your fists in front of your eyes and twist them to make a crying motion. When you get to the page where everyone is looking for Granny, pause briefly to let the children search for Granny in your storytime space. Once Granny is found, continue reading the story.

Spangler, Brie. *Peg Leg Peke.*

2008. New York: Alfred A. Knopf.

Summary: An off-page narrator convinces Peke, the Pekingese, to play pirate because his leg is in a cast.

Action: Before the start of the program, hide a bunch of different large paper letters throughout your storytime area. When you get to the part of the story where Peke drops anchor because he has spotted the "X" marking his treasure, stop reading so everyone can search for the "X" in your storytime area. Tell them to collect any letters that they find, but they should tell you when they find the "X." Continue the story once the "X" is found. After the story, identify the other letters that were found.

Stainton, Sue. *I Love Cats.*

2007. Illus., Anne Mortimer. New York: Katherine Tegen Books.

> **Summary:** A celebration of cats of all shapes and sizes.
>
> **Action:** The word *cats* appears 58 times in the text of this book. Each time that you read this word, have the children do a catlike motion. For example, they can make their hands paw-like by making fists and then opening them halfway. Have them use their "paws" to swat at imaginary bugs. To make the game more difficult, read the book quickly.

Stein, Peter. *Cars Galore.*

2011. Illus., Bob Staake. Somerville, MA: Candlewick Press.

> **Summary:** An action-packed verse about cars of all types.
>
> **Action:** Every time you read the word *car* or *cars* in this book, have the children hold their hands up like they are holding steering wheels. The word *car* or *cars* appears 58 times in the text. See who can keep up.

Taback, Simms. *Simms Taback's Safari Animals.*

2008. Maplewood, NJ: Blue Apple Books.

> **Summary:** Can you guess the animals before lifting all of the flaps?
>
> **Action:** Each animal starts with the words "Who am I?" and then give two clues before the animal is fully revealed. After each clue, have the children slap the floor with both hands like a drumroll. See who can guess the animal before the full picture is shown.

Thompson, Lauren. *Little Quack's Hide and Seek.*

2004. Illus., Derek Anderson. New York: Simon and Schuster Books for Young Readers.

> **Summary:** Little Quack and his siblings play hide-and-seek with their mother.
>
> **Action:** Hide five duck pictures or stuffed animals around your storytime space before the program starts. When Mama starts looking for her baby ducks, pause the story so everyone can search for the five baby ducks. Once all of the ducks are found, continue the story.

Timmers, Leo. *Who Is Driving?*

2005. New York: Bloomsbury Children's Books.

> **Summary:** Different animals drive one of seven vehicles to their own special location.

Action: Each vehicle starts with the words "Who is driving . . ." and shows four different animals in different clothing. Let the kids guess who is driving each vehicle before turning the page. Then have them move around the room like each vehicle before going on to the next guessing game:

- Fire engine—Move quickly around the room making a siren noise.
- Fancy car—Hold a pretend steering wheel and drive carefully around the room so you don't smudge the paint on the car.
- Race car—Hold your steering wheel tightly as you run around the room.
- Tractor—Bounce up and down while you walk around the room.
- Convertible—Pretend to roll back the top of the car from above you then drive around the room.
- Jeep—Hold the steering wheel and bounce around while you point at different imaginary animals that you see.
- Airplane—Hold your arms out like the wings of a plane and fly around the room.

Walsh, Melanie. *My Beak, Your Beak.*

2002. Boston: Houghton Mifflin.

Summary: Five pairs of animals are compared through their similarities and differences.

Action: Play a game to see who can guess the similarities between the two animals. For example, read the first two pages: "Dachshunds are long with little legs." "Dalmatians are tall and spotty. But . . ." Then let the kids guess which similarity the author chose. Before turning the page to find that dachshunds and Dalmatians "both love chasing sticks," have everyone hit the ground for a drumroll. Play the guessing game and do the drumroll for each pair of animals.

Wild, Margaret. *Piglet and Mama.*

2004. Illus., Stephen Michael King. New York: Harry N. Abrams.

Summary: Piglet loses her mother and asks all of the other farm animals for help finding her.

Action: Hide a pig puppet in your storytime space before the program begins. When you get to the page right before Piglet finds her mother, take a short break from reading and have everyone search your space for Piglet's mother. Once Mama has been found, continue with the rest of the story.

Yee, Brenda Shannon. *Hide and Seek.*

2001. Illus., Debbie Tilley. New York: Orchard Books.

Summary: A mouse plays hide-and-seek with an unsuspecting homeowner.

Action: Hide a stuffed mouse or picture of a mouse in your storytime space before the program begins. When you read the words "Ready or not! Here I come!" stop reading so everyone can search your storytime space for a mouse. When the mouse has been found, finish reading the book.

movement

Jumping and clapping! Who says you have to sit still during storytime? The books in this chapter are perfect for bouncing, stomping, and parading around the room. You can run in place every time a feisty puppy decides to run; bounce up and down with a bumpy wheelbarrow; or "Shhh" the room while animals try to sleep. You don't need special props or supplies. Follow the instructions provided for each title for an active and silly storytime. You may even find that everyone (adults included) gets a fun workout.

tips
- Ask the adults in the room to participate with their children.
- Do the movements along with the kids as much as possible. For example, when reading *Tall*, squish down toward the floor and stand up tall whenever you are asking the kids to do the same. They will understand the movements better if they are able to copy you. This is especially important for more difficult sequences such as the movements suggested for *Catalina Magdalena Hoopensteiner Wallendiner Hogan Logan Bogan Was Her Name*.

- Use a bell or other noisemaker to signal when it is time to stop moving and settle down for more of the book. This will be helpful when reading a book such as *How to Be*. Kids will also tend to follow you. If you are moving along with them, many of them will stop when you stop. Another idea is to have kids move for a count of five. While they move, you count out loud "One, Two, Three, Four, Five." When you say "Five," everyone should stop moving. Be sure to practice before reading the book.
- Practice doing the suggested movements. The kids dance a lot during *Rattlesnake Dance*. Practice dancing to those words before you start reading the book. Practice wiggling fingers and toes before you read *Ten Little Fingers and Ten Little Toes*.
- Use masking tape to make a circle for kids to stand on to help them form a circle as a group.
- It is okay for the kids to be up and moving during an entire book. During *Prancing Dancing Lily*, you want the kids to quietly dance throughout the whole book.
- For many of these stories, let the kids stand during the entire book. Some of the stories have so many movements that it will be easier to have them stand than make them sit down in between each movement. If the kids are standing, be sure to stand up, too, so that the kids can see the book.

Agee, Jon. *Z Goes Home.*

2003. New York: Hyperion Books for Children.

Summary: The letter Z passes other artistic letters on his way home from work.

Action: Since there isn't a story for this book, you can have the kids pretend to act out or do a movement for almost every letter:

- A—Alien: Walk like an alien.
- B—Bridge: Balance carefully as you walk across the bridge.
- C—Cake and D—Doughnut: Eat a piece of cake and a doughnut.
- E—Earthquake: Shake like an earthquake.
- F—Factory: Build something at the factory.
- G—Gargoyle: Stand perfectly still like a stone gargoyle.
- H—Hurdles: Jump over the hurdle.
- I—Ink: Write your name in the sky.
- J—Jetty: Pretend to walk a long distance out on the jetty.

- K—Karate: Do a karate chop.
- L—Labyrinth: Have the kids follow you through a labyrinth with lots of turns and dead ends.
- M—Mirror: Follow the leader in movements like a mirror.
- N—Newspaper: Read the newspaper.
- O—Oak and P—Palm: Stand tall like a tree.
- Q—Quicksand: Sink in the quicksand (pretend to sink into the floor).
- R—Rocks: Pick up a heavy rock.
- S—Seashore: Look for seashells on the seashore.
- T—Trophy: Hold your trophy high.
- U—Uniforms: Put on your clothes.
- V—Viper: Squirm on the ground like a snake.
- W—Woodpile: Stack wood in a pile.
- X—Xeroxes: Lift the cover of the Xerox machine and push the copy button.
- Y—Yoga: Do a yoga pose.

Alborough, Jez. *Tall.*

2005. Cambridge, MA: Candlewick Press.

Summary: A little monkey finds ways to make himself feel tall next to larger animals.

Action: Have the kids stand up when you start reading this book. Whenever you say "small," have them squish down and make themselves small. Whenever you say "tall," they should stand up straight and make themselves as tall as possible. They can even act out "fall" by falling on the ground.

Alborough, Jez. *Duck in the Truck.*

2008. La Jolla, CA: Kane/Miller Book.

Summary: Frog, Sheep, and Goat help Duck when his truck gets stuck in the muck.

Action: When Frog and Sheep try to push the truck out of the muck, have the kids pretend to push, too. When Goat helps by pulling on the truck, the kids can pretend to pull on a rope like they are playing tug-of-war.

alternate activity

Another option is to have one kid pretend to be the stuck truck and call up other kids to be Duck, Frog, Sheep, and Goat.

Andrews, Sylvia. *Dancing in My Bones.*

2001. Illus., Ellen Mueller. New York: HarperFestival.

Summary: Children dance, tap, bounce, sway, snap, clap, shake, and sing to the music in their heads.

Action: Sing this book to your own tune and act out all of the motions with the kids. For the page that reads "I've got music in my head, in my head . . . ," point to your head and shake it back and forth. For the page that reads "I've got singing in my mouth, in my mouth," add the words "La La" or other singing words at the end of each line.

Anholt, Laurence. *Chimp and Zee.*

2001. Illus., Catherine Anholt. New York: Phyllis Fogelman Books.

Summary: Monkeys Chimp and Zee go on a wild adventure while shopping for bananas with Mumkey.

Action: The words "Up jumps Chimp. Up jumps Zee" appear four times in the text. Every time you read those words, jump up and down with the kids.

Appelt, Kathi. *Bats Around the Clock.*

2000. Illus., Melissa Sweet. New York: HarperCollins.

Summary: Click Dark hosts American Batstand as the bats dance around the clock.

Action: Have the kids get up and dance throughout the book. They can do particular dances when they come up in the text (i.e., the swim, the locomotion, the twist, and the hokey pokey). If adults are in your storytime, be sure to include them in the fun.

Arnold, Marsha Diane. *Prancing Dancing Lily.*

2004. Illus., John Manders. New York: Dial Books for Young Readers.

Summary: Lily the dancing cow travels the world looking for a place to fit in and finds a way to fit in back at home.

Action: You can dance your way through this book. The kids can stand up and dance in place while you read. Especially focus on the conga line and have the kids do that when Lily discovers the dance.

Arnold, Tedd. *Catalina Magdalena Hoopensteiner Wallendiner Hogan Logan Bogan Was Her Name.*

2004. New York: Scholastic.

> **Summary:** A girl with a long and funny name grows up and eventually gets married.
>
> **Action:** Make up fun movements for the kids to go along with Catalina's name. For example, jump to the beat of "Catalina Magdalena," stomp to the beat of "Hoopensteiner Wallendiner," and clap to the beat of "Hogan Logan Bogan." Her name appears ten times in the text. By the end of the story, the kids will be worn out but will remember her name.

Arnosky, Jim. *Rattlesnake Dance.*

2000. New York: G. P. Putnam's Sons.

> **Summary:** Snakes join together to dance in the cool of the caves.
>
> **Action:** Whenever you read the words "Rattlesnake Dance," let the kids dance. You can use the instructions on the very last page: "You can do the rattlesnake dance too! Just hold your arms down to your sides and sway side to side like a snake." If you wish, you can use the musical score in the beginning of the book to sing the whole story.

Ashman, Linda. *Can You Make a Piggy Giggle?*

2002. Illus., Henry Cole. New York: Dutton Children's Books.

> **Summary:** A little boy does everything he can to make a pig laugh.
>
> **Action:** Have the children act out the motions along with the little boy: pretend to play a fiddle, waddle through a puddle, flap their arms and yodel, twirl around and tumble, stomp their feet and grumble, wriggle like a noodle, and polka with a poodle. Then have them try to do it all faster.

Aylesworth, Jim. *Little Bitty Mousie.*

2007. Illus., Michael Hague. New York: Walker.

> **Summary:** A little mouse sneaks into a house and explores through the alphabet.
>
> **Action:** Whenever you read the words "Tip-tip tippy tippy, Went her little mousie toes. Sniff-sniff sniffy sniffy, Went her little mousie nose," have the kids tiptoe around and then sniff the air. This stanza appears eight times in the text.

Ayres, Katherine. *Up, Down, and Around.*

2007. Illus., Nadine Bernard Westcott. Cambridge, MA: Candlewick Press.

Summary: Some edible plants grow up, some grow down, and some twine around.

Action: Have the kids stand up at the beginning of the book. When a plant grows up, they can reach tall in the air. When a plant grows down, they can squat down. When a plant twines around, they can spin in a circle.

Azarian, Mary. *A Gardener's Alphabet.*

2000. Boston: Houghton Mifflin.

Summary: Garden words for every letter of the alphabet are illustrated on their own page.

Action: Use your imagination to have the audience do movements for many of the pages in this book. Examples are:

- Bulbs—Plant some bulbs.
- Dig—Dig in the ground.
- Fountain—Splash in the fountain.
- Insects—Catch a friendly insect.
- Nibble—Nibble on yummy vegetables.
- Weed—Pull up the weeds.

Bates, Ivan, illus. *Five Little Ducks.*

2006. New York: Orchard Books.

Summary: An illustrated version of the classic song in which the mother duck's babies slowly disappear, but return in the end.

Action: Create motions that can be done while reading the story and have the children mimic your motions. When you read "over the hills and far away," go up and down a hill with your arm and then put your hand up to your forehead as you look far away. When the ducks come "waddling back," rock side to side on your feet as you pretend to waddle. Because the motions happen so often in this story, it is probably best to have the kids stand during the entire reading.

Bee, William. *Beware of the Frog.*

2008. Somerville, MA: Candlewick Press.

Summary: A pet frog protects a sweet little old lady from the Greedy Goblin, Smelly Troll, and Giant Hungry Ogre.

Action: The pet frog eats all of the bad guys in this story. Before you start reading the story, tell the kids about the phrase "But oh, dear, the frog doesn't look very pleased about that . . . ." When they hear the phrase, they should open their hands wide (one hand up and the other down) and "gobble" up the bad guy. Do this for all three bad guys and for the surprise ending when the sweet little old lady eats the frog.

Berry, Lynne. *Ducking for Apples.*

2010. Illus., Hiroe Nakata. New York: Henry Holt.

Summary: Five little ducks go for a bike ride and bring home apples for a snack.

Action: Oftentimes, all five ducks are doing something together, but sometimes only one, two, three, or four ducks are doing an action. Whenever the number of ducks is listed, count out that many ducks on your fingers with the kids in your program. For example: "One duck teeters," hold up one finger; "Two ducks swerve," hold up two fingers and count one-two; "Three ducks totter," hold up three fingers and count one-two-three.

Bond, Rebecca. *The Great Doughnut Parade.*

2007. Boston: Houghton Mifflin.

Summary: A young boy with a doughnut causes a merry parade.

Action: First tie a doughnut-shaped piece of paper around your waist. Walk around the room as you read the story. When you read "the doughnut brought a Hen, with a cluck! cluck! cluck!" have one child stand up and join your parade. When you read "then came the Cat, all quiet and slinky," add another child to your parade. As each character joins the parade, pull in another child. Eventually everyone in the room (perhaps adults included) will be parading around the room to the story. When Billy stops and there is clucking and leaping and barking, and so forth, let everyone dance and jump and laugh. Then have everyone sit down for the last couple of pages after Billy has left the parade.

Bowie, C.W. *Busy Fingers.*

2003. Illus., Fred Willingham. Watertown, MA: Whispering Coyote.

Summary: A rhyming depiction of many of the things fingers can do.

Action: Act out as many motions as possible in this book with the kids: hold your fingers high, hold them low, touch your toes, say "I love you" in sign language, wave goodbye, pretend to wash your hands, sing "The

Itsy Bitsy Spider," pretend to push a toy truck, count to three, pet an animal, poke at a sand castle, put toys away, take off socks, take a bath, dry off, rub tired eyes, and blow a kiss goodnight.

Brown, Lisa. *How to Be.*

2006. New York: HarperCollins.

Summary: Two children pretend to be a bear, monkey, turtle, snake, spider, and dog.

Action: Let the kids pretend to be each animal before you read about it. For example, when it says "How to be a BEAR," ask the kids to act like bears for a few seconds. Then have them sit down and read the four ways that the kids in the book pretend to be bears. Next, the book says "How to be a MONKEY." Let the kids pretend to be monkeys for a few seconds before you read the next couple of pages. Repeat this process for all of the animals in the book.

Bruel, Nick. *BOING.*

2004. Brookfield, CT: Roaring Brook Press.

Summary: A young kangaroo learns to jump with the help of his mother, a grasshopper, a frog, a rabbit, and a koala.

Action: The mother kangaroo, the grasshopper, the frog, the rabbit, and, finally, the joey all jump in this book. Whenever an animal jumps, the kids can jump along with them.

Burris, Priscilla. *Five Green and Speckled Frogs.*

2003. New York: Scholastic.

Summary: A retelling of the children's song where frogs eat bugs and jump into a cool pool.

Action: There are two easy motions to do while reading this book. Whenever the frogs eat bugs, the children can rub their stomachs and say "Yum yum." Whenever one of the frogs jumps into the pool, the children can plug their noses and jump.

Bush, Timothy, illus. *Teddy Bear, Teddy Bear.*

2005. New York: Greenwillow Books.

Summary: An illustrated version of the traditional nursery rhyme.

Action: Have the children follow along with the motions in this book: touch the ground, turn around, say hello, off you go, jump up high, touch the sky, go upstairs, say your prayers, turn out the light, and say goodnight. The very last page has helpful pictures for each of the actions.

Buzzeo, Toni. *Ready or Not, Dawdle Duckling.*

2005. Illus., Margaret Spengler. New York: Dial Books for Young Readers.

Summary: Dawdle Duckling gets help from his friends while playing hide-and-seek with his family.

Action: Mama Duck and her ducklings play hide-and-seek four times in this book. Each time, three of the ducklings hide very well. Whenever you read "One, two, three ducklings disappear," have the kids count one, two, three on their fingers and then hide that hand behind their backs. When you read "Ollie, ollie in free! One, two, three," bring the hidden "duckling fingers" back out.

Cabrera, Jane. *If You're Happy and You Know It!*

2003. New York: Holiday House.

Summary: Sing the classic song along with the animals in this book.

Action: Have the kids do the actions in the book as you read along: clap your hands, stamp your feet, nod your heads, roar out loud, spin around, go kiss kiss, flap your arms, say squeak squeak, jump around, and do them all together.

Carter, Don. *Get to Work Trucks!*

2002. Brookfield, CT: Roaring Brook Press.

Summary: Different types of construction equipment go to work.

Action: The kids can pretend to drive the equipment throughout the whole book. At the end of each page, have them put their hands up like they are holding steering wheels. They can turn their steering wheels and say "vroom-vroom" as they "drive" their trucks.

Church, Caroline Jayne. *Do Your Ears Hang Low?*

2001. New York: Scholastic.

Summary: A puppy-filled interpretation of the classic children's song.

Action: As you read the story, the children can act out the motions of the song. This book gives handy instructions for each movement on the back two pages. You don't need any special props, just your hands.

Clements, Andrew. *Slippers Loves to Run.*

2006. Illus., Janie Bynum. New York: Dutton Children's Books.

Summary: Slippers goes on an adventure and eventually runs home.

Action: The words *run* and *ran* are used a lot in this book. Have the kids stand up before you start reading. Tell them they will run in place every time you read the words *run* and *ran*. Practice doing so a couple of times. As you read the book, run in place with them every time the words appear.

Cotton, Cynthia. *Rain Play.*

2008. Illus., Javaka Steptoe. New York: Henry Holt.

Summary: A rainstorm comes, but that doesn't stop the children from playing.

Action: At the end of each page, have the children make rain with their fingers. Tell them to hold both hands out and flutter their fingers as they lower their hands.

Cronin, Doreen. *Bounce.*

2007. Illus., Scott Menchin. New York: Atheneum Books for Young Readers.

Summary: Bounce along with the animals in a variety of places.

Action: Ask the children to stand up. Tell them to jump every time you say the word *bounce.* Practice this a few times and then read the book and let them bounce along.

Dewdney, Anna. *Roly Poly Pangolin.*

2010. New York: Viking.

Summary: A roly poly pangolin is scared of the world until he finds a friend just like him.

Action: Before you start reading the story, show the kids how to roll their hands and wrists around each other just like when they sing "The Wheels on the Bus." Have them practice doing that every time you say "roly poly." The words *roly poly* appear 18 times in the text. As you read the story, do the motions each time you read it.

> **alternate books** Also check out the following two titles by the same author and illustrator for opportunities to wiggle and stretch through a book:
>
> **Cronin, Doreen. *Wiggle.*** 2005. Illus., Scott Menchin. New York: Atheneum Books for Young Readers.
>
> ———. ***Stretch.*** 2009. Illus., Scott Menchin. New York: Atheneum Books for Young Readers.

Edwards, Pamela Duncan. *McGillycuddy Could!*

2005. Illus., Sue Porter. New York: Katherine Tegen Books.

Summary: A kangaroo learns that it is not able to do normal farm activities, but it can still be helpful.

Action: In this book, McGillycuddy the kangaroo hops, jumps, bounces, and kicks. When you get to the part where McGillycuddy does any of those actions, have the kids join in. Be careful with the kicks so that no one gets hurt.

Fischer, Scott M. *Jump!*

2010. New York: Simon and Schuster Books for Young Readers.

Summary: A bug, frog, cat, hound, croc, and shark all jump to get away from an animal that is bigger than them.

Action: Have the kids jump along with the animals in the book. After a couple of pages, the kids will know exactly when the jump is coming because of the text: "Until I see a frog, and I . . . JUMP!" or "Until I see a cat, and I . . . JUMP!"

Fleming, Candace. *Muncha! Muncha! Muncha!*

2002. Illus., G. Brian Karas. New York: Atheneum Books for Young Readers.

Summary: Mr. McGreely unsuccessfully tries to keep bunnies out of his vegetable garden.

Action: The bunnies break into Mr. McGreely's garden multiple times throughout the book. Each time they enjoy the vegetables: "Muncha! Muncha! Muncha!" Whenever you read those words, have the kids rub their stomachs as if something is yummy.

Fox, Diane, and Christyan Fox. *Tyson the Terrible.*

2006. New York: Bloomsbury.

Summary: Stegg, Serra, and Plod are scared of Tyson the Terrible until they meet a small tyrannosaurus.

Action: Stegg, Serra, and Plod hear a faint booming sound that gets louder until they finally meet the small tyrannosaurus. Have the children stomp their feet throughout the book to mimic the sound. They can stop stomping on the page that starts with "'Nobody ever wants to play with me!' wailed a little voice." They can stomp one more time on the very last page when Stegg, Serra, and Plod finally meet Tyson.

Fox, Mem. *Ten Little Fingers and Ten Little Toes.*

2008. Illus., Helen Oxenbury. Orlando, Harcourt.

> **Summary:** Babies from all around the world have ten little fingers and ten little toes.
>
> **Action:** The words "And both of these babies, as everyone knows, had ten little fingers, and ten little toes" appears five times in the text. Each time you read those words, have the kids wiggle their fingers and then their toes.

Gran, Julia. *Big Bug Surprise.*

2007. New York: Scholastic Press.

> **Summary:** Prunella is eager to share her bugs in school and ends up saving the day.
>
> **Action:** The words "Not now, Prunella" appear five times in the text. Every time you read those words, have the children point their fingers and shake their hands as if they are disciplining someone.

Graves, Keith. *Chicken Big.*

2010. San Francisco: Chronicle Books.

> **Summary:** A large chick is born on a tiny farm and has to save the day before he is accepted by the other chickens.
>
> **Action:** The smallest chicken believes that the world is coming to an end three times in this book and everyone runs for their lives. Whenever that happens in the book, have the kids run really fast in place.

Hall, Algy Craig. *Fine as We Are.*

2008. New York: Boxer Books.

> **Summary:** A little frog and his mother are happy together until a bunch of tadpoles joins the family.
>
> **Action:** Have the kids act like frogs on each page of this book. Once you are done reading the page, show them how to jump up and down from a frog position: squat down bending their knees outward then put their hands on the floor in between their legs and jump.

Hamilton, Kersten. *Firefighters to the Rescue.*

2005. Illus., Rich Davis. New York: Viking.

> **Summary:** A crew of firefighters puts out a house fire and saves a dog.

Action: After reading each page of this book, have the kids act like they are driving fire trucks. Have them hold out their arms as if they are holding steering wheels and walk around making siren noises.

———. *Red Truck.*

2008. Illus., Valeria Petrone. New York: Viking.

Summary: A red tow truck saves a stuck school bus.

Action: After completing each page of this book, have the kids act like they are driving big trucks. Have them hold out their arms as if they are holding steering wheels and walk around making loud "vroom-vroom" noises.

Hilb, Nora, and Sharon Jennings. *Wiggle Giggle Tickle Train.*

2009. Illus., Nora and Marcela Cabezas Hilb. Toronto: Annick Press.

Summary: Children use their imaginations to interpret pictures of everyday things.

Action: Each double-page spread has a photograph on the left-hand side. As you flip each page, have the kids hold their hands up near their faces as if they are holding cameras. Have everyone say "click" and pretend to take a picture.

Hubbell, Patricia. *Airplanes: Soaring! Diving! Turning!*

2008. Illus., Megan Halsey and Sean Addy. Tarrytown, NY: Marshall Cavendish Children.

Summary: A description of all the different types of planes as they fly.

Action: Have the children hold out their arms like the wings on a plane. Let them take a few seconds to fly around the room after each page in this book.

---

alternate books Kids can also act like a truck, train, or car in these other books by the same author:

Hubbell, Patricia. *Trucks: Whizz! Zoom! Rumble!* *2003. Illus., Megan Halsey. Tarrytown, NY: Marshall Cavendish Children.*

———. *Trains: Steaming! Pulling! Huffing!* *2005. Illus., Megan Halsey and Sean Addy. Tarrytown, NY: Marshall Cavendish Children.*

———. *Cars: Rushing! Honking! Zooming!* *2006. Illus., Megan Halsey and Sean Addy. Tarrytown, NY: Marshall Cavendish Children.*

Hutchins, Pat. *Bumpety Bump!*

2006. New York: Greenwillow Books.

Summary: A boy and his grandfather gather food in the garden.

Action: The boy rides in the "bumpety bumpety bump" wheelbarrow. Whenever he is riding, bounce up and down with the children as you read.

Ichikawa, Satomi. *Come Fly with Me.*

2008. New York: Philomel Books.

Summary: A stuffed dog and toy plane go on a flying adventure together.

Action: The dog and the plane are flying through a majority of this story. Whenever they are flying, have the children hold their arms out like the wings of a plane and pretend to soar through the sky.

James, Simon. *Little One Step.*

2003. Cambridge, MA: Candlewick Press.

Summary: When the smallest duckling gets tired, his older brother teaches him to take it one step at a time.

Action: The smallest duckling plays a game called "One Step" to make it back to his mother. It is played by lifting your foot and saying "one" and then putting it down and saying "step." Those words appear numerous times in the text, as both the game and as a new nickname for the smallest duckling. Whenever you read those words, have the kids play "One Step."

Jarman, Julia. *Class Two at the Zoo.*

2007. Illus., Lynne Chapman. Minneapolis: Carolrhoda Books.

Summary: An anaconda swallows some students in Class Two during their visit to the zoo, but a savvy student saves them all.

Action: The anaconda eats seven students and the teacher. Each time another person is swallowed, have the children open their arms wide, then clap them together quickly. When everyone is saved because a stick holds open the snake's mouth, the children can hold their arms open until everyone crawls back out of the snake.

Johnson, Suzanne C. *Fribbity Ribbit!*

2001. Illus., Debbie Tilley. New York: Alfred A. Knopf.

Summary: A frog gets loose inside a house and causes a mess.

Action: The frog in this story hops around a lot and causes havoc. Have the kids jump like frogs at the end of every page.

Johnston, Lynn, and Beth Cruikshank. *Farley Follows His Nose.*
2009. Illus., Lynn Johnston. New York: The Bowen Press.
   Summary: Farley the dog has an adventure, gets lost, and saves the day by following his nose.
   Action: Farley is constantly sniffing the wonderful smells all around him in this story. Whenever he decides to follow his nose, have the children wiggle their noses and sniff the air.

Katz, Karen. *Mommy Hugs.*
2006. New York: Margaret K. McElderry Books.
   Summary: Mommy hugs baby many times throughout the day.
   Action: Mommy hugs baby one time on the first page. Have the children wrap their arms around themselves and give themselves one hug. On the second page, mommy gives baby two hugs. Again have the children give themselves a hug, but this time count "one, two" and squeeze twice. Continue until mommy gives ten hugs to baby on the last page.

Kelly, Mij. *William and the Night Train.*
2000. Illus., Alison Jay. New York: Farrar Straus Giroux.
   Summary: The night train waits for wide-awake William to sleep so it can take everyone to tomorrow.
   Action: Focus on the bedtime train part of this story. After every page, have the kids bend their arms and move them like train wheels and then yawn so they can help William settle down enough to sleep.

Kirk, Daniel. *Bus Stop, Bus Go!*
2001. New York: G. P. Putnam's Sons.
   Summary: Tommy's pet hamster gets loose on a school bus on the way to school.
   Action: The words "Bus stop, bus go!" appear eight times in this text. When you read "Bus stop," everyone should stand very still. When you read "Bus go," everyone should run in place until you say stop again. The kids will be moving throughout most of the book.

Kirk, Daniel. *Honk Honk! Beep Beep!*

2010. New York: Disney Hyperion Books.

Summary: A little boy and his father meet many friends as they drive off to watch the sunrise.

Action: The words "Honk Honk! Beep Beep!" appear seven times in the text. Every time you read those words, have the kids press the horn twice with their hands for "Honk Honk!" and stamp their feet twice for "Beep Beep!"

Koller, Jackie French. *Seven Spunky Monkeys.*

2005. Illus., Lynn Munsinger. Orlando: Harcourt.

Summary: Seven monkeys go out on Sunday and by the end of the week each of them has left the group to fall in love.

Action: When there are seven spunky monkeys in the group, count up to seven on your fingers and have the kids hold up that number until one of the monkeys falls in love. Then as a group lower one finger and count to six together and keep reading. Continue until you aren't holding up any more fingers.

Lakin, Patricia. *Rainy Day!*

2007. Illus., Scott Nash. New York: Dial Books for Young Readers.

Summary: Sam, Pam, Will, and Jill find fun things to do inside and outside on a rainy day.

Action: Have the kids create rain on each page as you read the story. To create rain, have them hold their hands out straight. Show them how to wiggle their fingers as they slowly lower their hands to simulate rain falling down.

Leuck, Laura. *Goodnight, Baby Monster.*

2002. Illus., Nigel McMullen. New York: HarperCollins.

Summary: Mothers tuck in their spooky and nighttime babies.

Action: Each monster is tucked in with two lines in the text. For example: "Goodnight, baby monster, all warm in your den." After each animal, have everyone say "Shhh" and pretend to tuck in the monster or animal.

Lewin, Betsy. *Where Is Tippy Toes?*

2010. New York: Atheneum Books for Young Readers.

Summary: A cat named Tippy Toes is easy to find during the day, but only one person knows where he goes at night.

Action: Tippy Toes is a cute and funny name for a cat. Have the kids walk on their tiptoes every time you read the name Tippy Toes.

Lillegard, Dee. *Balloons Balloons Balloons.*

2007. Illus., Bernadette Pons. New York: Dutton Children's Books.

Summary: The whole rabbit town gets a pleasant surprise when balloons show up everywhere.

Action: The words "Snap snap, Clap clap, Balloons Balloons Balloons" appear three times in the text. Every time you read those words, have the children snap twice, clap twice, and then raise their arms as if they are saying "hooray" three times. There are also many places where just the words "Balloons Balloons Balloons" appear. Do the "hooray" motion each time you read that as well. If you wish to add more movement, they can raise their arms every time the word *balloons* appears (55 times!).

Livingston, Irene. *Finklehopper Frog.*

2003. Illus., Brian Lies. Berkeley, CA: Tricycle Press.

Summary: Finklehopper wants to jog with everyone else and realizes it is okay that he only hops.

Action: Finklehopper Frog puts on his new jogging suit and goes out to run, but instead he hips and hops down the road. Have everyone jump and hop like a frog with Finklehopper for the rest of the book as Finklehopper exercises the best way for him.

London, Jonathan. *A Train Goes Clickety-Clack.*

2007. Illus., Denis Roche. New York: Henry Holt.

Summary: A description of different types of trains.

Action: At the end of every page, have the children bend their arms and move them like the wheels on a train. For extra effect, they can add train sound effects such as "chugga chugga" and "woo woo."

Loomis, Christine. *Scuba Bunnies.*

2004. Illus., Ora Eitan. New York: G. P. Putnam's Sons.

Summary: Rabbits scuba dive to explore sea creatures and sunken treasure.

Action: The rabbits are exploring under the sea through a majority of this book. At the end of any page where they are scuba diving, have the children pretend to swim along with them.

MacDonald, Margaret Read. *A Hen, a Chick, and a String Guitar.*

2005. Illus., Sophie Fatus. Cambridge, MA: Barefoot Books.

Summary: Different family members give a boy many farm animals and soon all sixteen are dancing.

Action: Each time the boy gets a new animal, he lists all of his animals and says "Ay! Ay! Ay! Ay! Ay! How I loved my (# of animals) little pets!" Create a motion to do with the words "Ay! Ay! Ay! Ay! Ay!" For example, you can clap five times, jump five times, or dance to the words. Have the children do this motion each time the boy says those words.

Mandine, Selma. *Kiss Kiss.*

2009. Michelle Williams, trans. New York: Golden Books.

Summary: There are many different kinds of kisses from family and pets.

Action: At the end of every page, ask everyone to pucker up and "kiss kiss" the air.

Markes, Julie. *Shhhhh! Everybody's Sleeping.*

2005. Illus., David Parkins. New York: HarperCollins.

Summary: People with many different jobs are sleeping, but the child is still awake.

Action: Every page spread features a person with a different job who is sleeping. At the beginning of every page, have the children put their fingers up to their lips and say "Shhh."

Marlow, Layn. *Hurry Up and Slow Down.*

2008. New York: Holiday House.

Summary: Tortoise takes things slow, Hare likes to go fast, but they both take time to enjoy a story.

Action: Whenever you are reading about tortoise, read the words very slowly. Have the kids stand up and move around very slowly during those parts. Whenever you are reading about hare, read very quickly. Have the kids move very quickly to those parts. You don't have to specify how the kids move, just ask them to jump, or wiggle, or move their arms, and so forth.

Mayo, Margaret. *Choo Choo Clickety-Clack!*
2004. Illus., Alex Ayliffe. Minneapolis, MN: Carolrhoda Books.

Summary: A rhythmic description of many forms of transportation.

Action: Have the kids pretend to move like the many forms of transportation in this book:

- Trains—Bend your arms and move them in circles like the wheels on a train.
- Airplanes—Hold your arms out straight to the sides and pretend to soar through the air.
- Cars—Hold your arms out straight like you are holding a steering wheel and move around the room.
- Race cars—Hold your arms out straight like you are holding a steering wheel and run quickly in place.
- Sailboats—Sway back and forth like you are riding the waves in a boat.
- Hot-air balloons—Hold your arms straight up and sway them back and forth in the wind.
- Motorbikes—Hold your arms out like you are holding handlebars and flick your wrists like you are revving the engines.
- Bikes—Hold your arms out like you are holding handlebars and pretend to peddle with your legs.
- Cable cars—Pretend to shut the door of the cable car and look down as if the ground is far away.
- Buses—Pretend to use the lever to open the door for passengers and then pretend to hold the steering wheel.
- Ferryboats—Hold your arms out wide as if you are holding a large steering wheel for a boat.

McCarty, Peter. *Moon Plane.*
2006. New York: Henry Holt.

Summary: A young boy sees a plane in the air and dreams about riding in a plane to the moon.

Action: At the end of each page of this story, have the children put their arms out to the sides and pretend to fly like airplanes. At the end of the story, when the boy returns to Earth, the children can softly land their planes by sitting down.

McDonnell, Flora. *Giddy-Up! Let's Ride!*

2002. Cambridge, MA: Candlewick Press.

Summary: Ride along on a horse, elephant, camel, and unicorn.

Action: Ride along with the children throughout this book. After you finish reading each page, have everyone pretend to gallop around the room for a few seconds. If you want to be more inventive, you can ask everyone to try to imitate the rider on each page: twirl your lasso with the cowgirl, ride fast with the jockey, and stand tall and pretty with the fairy.

McNaughton, Colin. *Not Last Night But the Night Before.*

2009. Illus., Emma Chichester Clark. Somerville, MA: Candlewick Press.

Summary: Many childhood characters come knocking on the door of this little boy's house.

Action: On every page until near the end, a character knocks on the door. Whenever you read "came knocking at the door," have the children knock on the floor as if they are knocking on the door.

Meyers, Susan. *Puppies! Puppies! Puppies!*

2005. Illus., David Walker. New York: Henry N. Abrams.

Summary: Puppies of all shapes and sizes make friends and find families.

Action: The words "Here and there and everywhere, Puppies! Puppies! Puppies" appear six times throughout the book. When you read the word *puppies* three times in a row, have the children shake their tails (their bottoms) and bark three times.

Myers, Walter Dean. *Looking Like Me.*

2009. Illus., Christopher Myers. New York: Egmont.

Summary: Jeremy finds all of the people in his life that make him a brother, son, city child, dancer, and more.

Action: Whenever Jeremy talks to other people in this story, they each put out a fist and he gives "it a bam!" Whenever you read those words, have everyone make a fist and fist-bump the air. You can also have kids fist-bump one another.

Panahi, H. L. *Bebop Express.*

2005. Illus., Steve Johnson and Lou Fancher. New York: Laura Geringer Books.

Summary: A rhythmic train ride celebrates the jazz culture in the United States.

Action: There are many instances in this book where sounds are depicted using words. "Chug-a chug-a chug-a chug-a Choo! Choo! Chug-a chug-a chug-a chug-a Choo! Choo!" appears many times in this story. Whenever you read those words, have everyone dance to the beat. For extra action, have everyone dance to the sounds of the saxophone, drums, bass, and song. Or, read the whole story to a rhythmic beat and have people dance the whole way through.

Park, Linda Sue. *Bee-Bim Bop!*

2005. Illus., Ho Baek Lee. New York: Clarion Books.

Summary: A young girl helps her mother with the shopping and preparation of her favorite food.

Action: The words "BEE-BIM BOP!" appear seven times in the text. Those words create a fantastic rhythm. Every time you read those words, have everyone clap three times to the rhythm.

Paul, Ann Whitford. *Mañana Iguana.*

2004. Illus., Ethan Long. New York: Holiday House.

Summary: A new version of the Little Red Hen where Iguana does all of the work because Tortoise, Rabbit, and Snake won't help. Includes words in Spanish.

Action: Teach the children to act out the reasons that Rabbit, Tortoise, and Snake will not help Iguana. Whenever Rabbit/Conejo says he is too fast, run very quickly in place. Whenever Tortoise/Tortuga says he is too slow, pretend to walk very, very slowly. Whenever Snake/Culebra says he can't help because he doesn't have arms, stand very straight with your arms down at your sides.

Paxton, Tom. *The Marvelous Toy.*

2009. Illus., Steve Cox. New York: Imagine.

Summary: Three generations enjoy a strange toy even though they aren't sure what it is.

Action: In this story, the toy "went zip! when it moved and bop! when it stopped and whirr! when it stood still." Create motions to go along with the toy and have the children mimic your motions. When the toy goes "zip," quickly put both arms up into the air. When the toy goes "bop," jump once. When the toy goes "whirr," shake your whole body. Do these motions every time the toy is described this way throughout the book. The text of this book is a song, so you may choose to sing it rather than read it.

Pearson, Debora. *Sophie's Wheels.*

2006. Illus., Nora Hilb. Toronto: Annick Press.

Summary: Sophie grows through many sets of wheels: baby buggy, stroller, wagon, tricycle, and more.

Action: Help all of Sophie's wheels roll throughout the story. Have the children roll their wrists like they would for the "Wheels on the Bus" song after reading each page.

Peddicord, Jane Ann. *That Special Little Baby.*

2007. Illus., Meilo So. Orlando: Harcourt.

Summary: A little baby learns about the world and grows into a toddler.

Action: Each stanza of this book ends with the words "and grew and grew and grew!" Each time that you read these words, have the children crouch down really small and then "grow" three times until they are standing straight and tall. Here is one way for them to "grow": After the first "grew," their legs should be straight, but they should still be bent over at the waist. After the second "grew," they should be standing tall. After the last "grew," their hands should be reaching for the ceiling.

Pham, Leuyen. *Big Sister, Little Sister.*

2005. New York: Hyperion Books for Children.

Summary: A comparison of big and little sisters from the point of view of the little sister.

Action: Whenever you say something about the big sister, have everyone stand up very tall and big. Whenever you read something about the little sister, have everyone crouch down and make themselves very small. This book bounces back and forth many times between the two sisters so everyone will be moving a lot.

Polacco, Patricia. *Mommies Say Shhh!*

2005. New York: Philomel Books.

Summary: Animals make many different noises, bunnies say nothing at all, and mommies quiet them all down.

Action: The words "bunnies say nothing at all" appear four times in this book. Every time you read those words, have the children hold two fingers up on each hand and hold their hands behind the top of their heads like bunny ears. They can jump up and down and twitch their noses like bunnies.

Prince, April Jones. *What Do Wheels Do All Day?*

2006. Illus., Giles Laroche. Boston: Houghton Mifflin.

Summary: Wheels push, tow, whiz, spin, zoom, and more.

Action: The word *wheels* appears 22 times in the text. Every time you read that word, have everyone roll their arms as if they are singing "The Wheels on the Bus."

Raschka, Chris. *Little Black Crow.*

2010. New York: Atheneum Books for Young Readers.

Summary: A young boy wonders about the life of a crow: where does it sleep; where does it go when it snows?

Action: At the end of every page, have the children hold their arms out straight to the sides and flap their wings like crows. They can also caw like crows to add sound.

Ray, Mary Lyn. *Red Rubber Boot Day.*

2000. Illus., Lauren Stringer. San Diego: Harcourt.

Summary: On a rainy day, a little boy plays inside until he decides to put on his boots and play in the rain.

Action: While the boy plays inside, have the children pretend to make rain after reading each page. Tell them to hold their arms out straight and wiggle their fingers as they lower their arms to make rain. When the boy finally goes outside with his boots on, the children can pretend to bounce and jump in the puddles after each page.

Reiser, Lynn. *Hardworking Puppies.*

2006. Orlando: Harcourt.

> **Summary:** Ten puppies play together, but decide that each of them needs to find a job.

> **Action:** At the beginning of the story, there are ten puppies. Have everyone hold up ten fingers. When the first puppy finds a job with a firefighter, have everyone lower one finger and count the remaining nine fingers. When the second puppy finds a job with a lifeguard, have everyone lower another finger and count the remaining eight fingers. Continue until no one is holding up any fingers.

Roberts, Bethany. *Cat Skidoo.*

2004. Illus., R. W. Alley. New York: Henry Holt.

> **Summary:** Two kittens have an active day outside their house.

> **Action:** The words "Cat Skidoo!" appear eight times in this book. Every time you read those words, have the children do the following motions: For the word *cat,* they can pretend to pull on whiskers on either side of their faces. For the word *skidoo,* they can throw their arms up in the air as if they are saying "hooray!"

Rockliff, Mara. *Next to an Ant.*

2004. Illus., Pascale Constantin. New York: Children's Press.

> **Summary:** Any object can be tall when compared to something smaller than it.

> **Action:** Start out this book while crouching on the floor, and encourage the children to join you. As you read each page and discover that each object is taller than something else, slowly start to stand up. On the last page—"I am the tallest one of all!"—you and the children should be standing tall with your hands reaching into the sky.

Rockwell, Anne. *Here Comes the Night.*

2006. New York: Henry Holt.

> **Summary:** The whole world is getting ready to sleep as a mother eases her child into bed.

> **Action:** As Mother says goodnight, she also calms the evening by saying "Shhh." Whenever you read that word in the text, have the children raise their fingers to their mouths and say "Shhh" and then lay their heads on their hands as if they are going to sleep.

Ryder, Joanne. *Wild Birds.*

2003. Illus., Susan Estelle Kwas. New York: HarperCollins.

Summary: Wild birds are all around us throughout the year.

Action: At the end of every page, the children can flap their arms like they are wild birds.

Ryder, Joanne. *Won't You Be My Hugaroo?*

2006. Illus., Melissa Sweet. Orlando: Harcourt.

Summary: There are lots of different hugs to give at the right times.

Action: The word *hug* appears 18 times in the text (sometimes as part of other words such as *hugaroo*). Every time you read that word, pause briefly to allow the children to wrap their arms around themselves to give themselves a hug.

Salerno, Steven. *Harry Hungry!*

2009. Orlando: Harcourt.

Summary: Harry is so hungry that he finishes all the food in his house and then moves on to bigger things outside.

Action: Harry eats a lot of crazy things in this story (a mailbox, the neighbor's house, the highway). Every time Harry eats something, the children can rub their stomachs and say "Yum Yum."

Schertle, Alice. *Very Hairy Bear.*

2007. Illus., Matt Phelan. Orlando: Harcourt.

Summary: A very hairy bear does not mind that there isn't any hair on his nose until it gets cold out.

Action: The bear's nose is referred to nine times in the text. Every time you read the word *nose,* have the children rub the bridge of their noses (to make sure there isn't any hair). At the end of the story, have them cover their noses up with both of their hands so they will be warm like the bear's nose.

Schwartz, Amy. *A Beautiful Girl.*

2006. New Milford, CT: Roaring Brook Press.

Summary: On her way to the market, Jenna meets an elephant, a robin, a fly, and a goldfish and explains to them how she is different from them.

Action: As Jenna meets each animal, they comment on her trunk (nose), beak (mouth), 100 eyes (two eyes), and gills (ears). When Jenna corrects the animals and explains the names of her body parts, have the kids point to those parts on their bodies.

Seaworthy, Oscar. *Port Side Pirates!*

2007. Illus., Debbie Harter. Cambridge, MA: Barefoot Books.

Summary: A young boy sails away with fun pirates.

Action: This whole book can be sung and the chorus appears on each page. Create a dance for the children to do with the chorus. For example: "Oh we go this way" (hold their hands up to their foreheads and look off in the distance to the right), "that way" (keep holding their hands up and look to the left), "port side" (step to the left), "starboard" (step to the right), "over the deep blue sea!" (put their hands side by side and swim over the waves).

Seeger, Laura Vaccaro. *First the Egg.*

2007. New Milford, CT: Roaring Brook Press.

Summary: What comes first? The chicken or the egg? The frog or the tadpole?

Action: This book shows many transformations in the world. For each one, the book states "First the x" and then on the next page "then the y." The kids can add to the suspense of the book by raising their hands in the air and shaking them (like clapping in American Sign Language). For example: "First the EGG," shake hands in the air, "then the CHICKEN."

Serfozo, Mary. *Whooo's There?*

2007. Illus., Jeffrey Scherer. New York: Random House.

Summary: An inquisitive owl discovers who else is awake during the night.

Action: The owl says "Whooo" many times to find out who else is out in the night. Every time you read the word *whooo,* have the children use the fingers on both of their hands to make two "O" shapes, and then hold the circles up to their eyes so they have great big owl eyes, too. Have everyone say "Whooo" with the owl.

Sharkey, Niamh. *The Ravenous Beast.*

2003. Cambridge, MA: Candlewick Press.

Summary: Various animals from a mouse to a whale try to prove that they are hungrier than the previous animal.

Action: The word *hungry* is used many times in this book. Every time you read the word *hungry,* the children can rub their stomachs as if they are hungry.

Sherry, Kevin. *I'm the Biggest Thing in the Ocean.*

2007. New York: Dial Books for Young Readers.

Summary: A giant squid thinks he is the biggest thing in the ocean until he gets swallowed by a whale.

Action: At the beginning of the story, have the kids squish down near the floor to make themselves as small as possible. As the squid claims to be bigger than each animal, the kids can slowly start standing up and putting their arms out to make themselves bigger and bigger. When the whale finally comes along and eats the squid, the kids can hold one arm up and the other down and chomp down on the squid.

Steggall, Susan. *Rattle and Rap.*

2008. London: Frances Lincoln Children's Books.

Summary: Riders take a journey on a train to the seaside.

Action: This book is full of the noises and motions of a train. Have the children get in a circle and then put their hands on the shoulders of the person to their right to form a train. You should stand in the middle of the circle. After you read each page and show the picture to everyone, have the train move forward a few steps while you say "Chugga Chugga Choo Choo!"

Sturges, Philemon. *I Love Planes!*

2003. New York: HarperCollins.

Summary: A child loves all different types of planes.

Action: Since this book is about planes, have the kids pretend to fly like airplanes after you read each page. They can hold out their arms like the wings of a plane and walk around the room for a few seconds at the end of each page.

Thomas, Scott. *The Yawn Heard 'Round the World.*

2003. Illus., Tatjana Mai-Wyss. Berkeley, CA: Tricycle Press.

Summary: When one little girl yawns, it sets off a chain reaction of yawns around the world.

Action: Whenever a person or animal yawns in this book, have the children hold their arms up above their heads and stretch as they yawn.

Todd, Mark. *Monster Trucks!*

2003. Boston: Houghton Mifflin.

Summary: Big trucks such as garbage trucks, bulldozers, and plows do heavy work.

Action: Each page of this book starts with the words "Monster trucks! Monster trucks!" Each time you read those words, have the children hold onto their pretend steering wheels and say "vroom-vroom." Because these are really big trucks, the children should use deep, low voices.

Underwood, Deborah. *The Quiet Book.*

2010. Illus., Renata Liwska. Boston: Houghton Mifflin Books for Children.

Summary: An exploration of the many different kinds of quiet.

Action: Each page of this book shows a different type of quiet. At the end of each type, have the children hold their fingers up to their mouths and say "Shhh" to add to the quiet.

Vail, Rachel. *Righty and Lefty: A Tale of Two Feet.*

2007. Illus., Matthew Cordell. New York: Scholastic Press.

Summary: The right foot and the left foot have each other to play with but they don't always agree.

Action: This book switches back and forth between Righty and Lefty many times. Before you start reading the book, review left and right with everyone by holding up your left foot and then your right foot. Since you are standing in front of the group, you may want to hold up the opposite foot because the kids will copy you. Then every time you read about Righty, have the children hold their right feet up in the air. Every time you read about Lefty, have them hold their left feet up in the air.

Vamos, Samantha R. *The Cazuela That the Farm Maiden Stirred.*

2011. Illus., Rafael López. Watertown, MA: Charlesbridge.

Summary: A cumulative tale about a farm maiden who makes rice pudding with the help of some animals.

Action: Stir the arroz con leche (rice pudding) along with the farm maiden. Whenever she stirs the cazuela, have the children hold one arm out and move it in a circle as if they are stirring something in a very large bowl.

Weaver, Tess. *Cat Jumped In!*

2007. Illus., Emily Arnold McCully. New York: Clarion Books.

Summary: A curious cat jumps into a house and makes a mess everywhere he goes.

Action: Whenever the cat makes a mess, the homeowner yells at the cat to get out. Every time this happens, the cat quickly runs off to another part of the house. Whenever the cat runs away, have the children run quickly in place along with him.

Wild, Margaret. *Kiss Kiss!*

2003. Illus., Bridget Strevens-Marzo. New York: Simon and Schuster Books for Young Readers.

Summary: Baby Hippo goes off to play without kissing her mother, but realizes what she forgot when she sees other animals kissing their mothers.

Action: Whenever the animals in this book give their mothers a kiss, have the children create a kiss with their two hands by putting the tips of all of their fingers together on one hand and then doing the same with the other. Then have them put their hands together so that the fingertips "kiss" each other.

Willans, Tom. *Wait! I Want to Tell You a Story.*

2004. New York: Simon and Schuster Books for Young Readers.

Summary: A muskrat tricks a tiger by telling a story until a crocodile eats the tiger and the muskrat gets away.

Action: Muskrat tells a story in which numerous animals escape being eaten by saying "Wait! I want to tell you a story." Every time you read those words, have the kids throw their hands up in the air as if they are trying to get someone to stop.

Willems, Mo. *Don't Let the Pigeon Drive the Bus!*

2003. New York: Hyperion Books for Children.

———. *Don't Let the Pigeon Stay Up Late!*

2006. New York: Hyperion Books for Children.

Summary: A determined pigeon tries to convince the reader to let him drive the bus (or stay up late) even though he isn't allowed.

Action: Since the pigeon character is talking directly to the reader/listener, play along with the story. On each page, the pigeon tries another way of convincing you to let him drive the bus (or stay up late). Each time, have the children say "No!" loudly and shake their fingers back and forth for emphasis.

Williams, Karen Lynn. *A Beach Tail.*

2010. Illus., Floyd Cooper. Honesdale, PA: Boyds Mills Press.

Summary: Gregory travels a long way down the beach as he adds a long tail to his lion picture in the sand and has to follow the tail back to find his father.

Action: This activity works best in a large storytime space. When Gregory starts adding a long tail to his lion picture, tape down the end of a piece of string onto the floor near you. As you read the story, make a path on the floor with the string. You will want to tape down parts of the string every few feet or so. When Gregory realizes that he has to follow the tail to get back to his father, have all of the kids line up at the far end of your path and follow the string back to your starting point. You can also create a path on your floor using tape before the program starts to make this activity more manageable for the reader.

Willis, Jeanne. *Never Too Little to Love.*

2005. Illus., Jan Fearnley. Cambridge, MA: Candlewick Press.

Summary: A little mouse climbs on more and more items trying to reach his giraffe friend so he can give her a kiss.

Action: As the mouse piles up more and more objects trying to reach his friend, let the children try to stretch themselves taller and taller. When the objects crash under mouse, the children can fall on the floor (like they are playing "Ring Around the Rosey").

Wilson, Karma. *A Frog in the Bog.*

2003. Illus., Joan Rankin. New York: Margaret K. McElderry Books.

Summary: A frog eats so many bugs that he attracts the attention of a crocodile that wants to eat him.

Action: When you start reading this story, have the children crouch down on the floor to make themselves very small. As the frog eats more and more bugs, the children slowly stand up to make themselves bigger and bigger. When all of the bugs escape from the frog's stomach, the children crouch down to make themselves very small again.

———. *Bear Feels Sick.*

2007. Illus., Jane Chapman. New York: Margaret K. McElderry Books.

Summary: Bear feels sick but his friends take care of him until he feels better.

Action: Pretend to be sick along with Bear. Whenever you read the words "the bear feels sick" or "he still feels sick," have the children pretend to sneeze.

Wormell, Mary. *Why Not?*

2000. New York: Farrar Straus Giroux.

Summary: A mischievous kitten is warned to not scare the other animals on the farm.

Action: Whenever his mother tells him not to do something, Barnaby asks "WHY NOT?" Each time he does this, have the children ask the question along with him by putting their palms up in the air and shrugging their shoulders while they say the words.

Yee, Wong Herbert. *Who Likes Rain?*

2007. New York: Henry Holt.

Summary: A young girl explores outside during a rainstorm.

Action: Rain is falling during most of this book. On each page with rain, have the children make rain with their fingers. They can hold their arms straight out and wiggle their fingers as they lower their arms. On the very last page, they can pretend to jump in a puddle with the young girl.

Yolen, Jane. *How Do Dinosaurs Say I Love You?*

2009. Illus., Mark Teague. New York: The Blue Sky Press.

Summary: Little dinosaurs sometimes get into trouble, but they are always loved by their mothers and fathers.

Action: Whenever the dinosaurs misbehave, they do something good afterward and their parents tell them how much they love them. Whenever their parents tell their dinosaur that they love them, have the children give themselves a hug.

Yorinks, Arthur. *Happy Bees!*

2005. Illus., Carey Armstrong-Ellis. New York: Harry N. Abrams.

Summary: Bees live a carefree life while everyone around them tries to get rid of them.

Action: Have the children pretend to fly like a happy bee around the room every time you read the words "happy bees." They can point one finger out straight and wave their hands around in the air while they smile and make a buzzing sound.

Zane, Alexander. *The Wheels on the Race Car.*

2005. Illus., James Warhola. New York: Orchard Books.

Summary: A twist on the familiar children's song using race cars.

Action: Have the children sing the song and do motions for each verse (the endpapers of the hardcover edition show suggested movements):

- "wheels on the race car go round and round"—Circle your wrists around each other as you would for the "Wheels on the Bus" song, or follow the suggestion in the book and point a finger on each hand and make circles in the air.
- "engine in the race goes vroom-vroom-vroom"—Make fists with each hand and move your wrists up and down like you are revving the engine of a motorcycle.
- "driver in the race car yells, 'go-go-go'"—Point one finger on each hand and point back and forth.
- "race car on the track goes zip-zip-zip"—Put one hand out with your palm down and wave it side to side in front of you.
- "driver in the race car steers and steers"—Hold your hands out and pretend to hold a steering wheel that you are turning side to side.

- "race car mechanics go zizz-zizz-zizz"—Hold your hands together with your thumbs and pointer fingers pointing out together and pretend to use an impact wrench to put tires on the car.
- "gas from the gas can goes glug-glug-glug"—Pretend your whole body is the gas can and sway side to side to empty gas into the car.
- "driver in the race car speeds on back"—Stick your thumb out and move it like you are directing someone to go to the back.
- "driver in the race car makes his move"—Hold the steering wheel again and pretend to pass someone in front of you.
- "driver in the race car zooms to the lead"—Hold your hands out near your body and quickly straighten both arms up into the air like you are zooming to the moon.
- "checkered flag goes swish-swish-swish"—Hold both hands up in the air and wave them back and forth.
- "wheels on the race car go round and round"—Do the same motion as the first verse.

Zolotow, Charlotte. *Do You Know What I'll Do?*

2000. Illus., Javaka Steptoe. New York: HarperCollins.

Summary: A girl tells her younger brother how much she loves him by her actions.

Action: At the very end of the story, the girl gives her brother a great big hug. Ask everyone to walk up to a family member or friend in the room and give them a great big hug.

music

Musical tracks and maracas! Get ready to dance and make music. Don't worry about your dancing skills; the kids don't care. Just play some music at the end of each musical page and move to the beat. If the characters in the story are playing an instrument, play along with them. You'll also find many books in this chapter with rhythmic language. Pick your favorite instrument and play along to the beat. So get out those bells and maracas and make some music in the library.

tips

- Ask the adults in the room to participate with their children. If you are handing out musical instruments, give one to each adult if you have enough.
- Practice playing the instruments together before reading the book. If you want the kids to stop playing the instruments after a certain period of time, put your instrument on your lap or behind your back when it is time to stop. If the kids are playing instruments to a particular set of words, practice this before you read.

- Use masking tape to create a circle on the floor for books such as *Parade Day: Marching Through the Calendar Year*. Ask the kids to stand on the tape to create a quick circle. You can also use a round or oval rug and ask the kids to stand on the edge. Even a square or rectangle rug will work in a pinch.
- Practice moving when the music is playing and stopping when the music stops. Practice a few times before reading the book.
- Model playing and moving with the music throughout the book. Most of the kids will follow your lead.
- Sometimes the best idea is to have the kids put their instruments on the floor in between playing times. It is easier not to shake a bell that is not in your hand.
- If you are handing out different types of instruments, such as in *Look Out, Suzy Goose,* give kids sitting near each other the same instruments. Tell the kids to play their instrument only if you are standing in front of their group. Again, practice before you read.
- Remember that the kids might not play their instruments exactly to the beat. This is a learned skill that they will acquire over time as you practice more.
- Include clean-up time at the end of any story with a musical instrument. Ask the kids to return their instruments to your bag or container while you play music.

Anderson, Peggy Perry. *Chuck's Band.*

2008. Boston: Houghton Mifflin.

   Summary: Chuck and his farm animals make music together.

   Action: Hand out musical instruments at the beginning of the story. Have the kids play their instruments at the end of each page. Practice having them play for a count of three each time so that it is easier to move on to the next page.

Archambault, John. *Boom Chicka Rock.*

2004. Illus., Suzanne Tanner Chitwood. New York: Philomel Books.

   Summary: Twelve mice dance and rock around while the cat is asleep.

   Action: Give the kids instruments that they can shake and rattle every time you say "Boom Chicka Rock, Chicka Rock, Chicka Boom!" This phrase repeats four times in the text, but you can say it after every page. Also, this text lends itself to being read to a beat. Let the audience clap along.

Baker, Keith. *Hickory Dickory Dock.*

2007. Orlando: Harcourt.

Summary: The popular nursery rhyme is continued through 12 o'clock.

Action: Give the kids shakers at the beginning of the book. Have them shake the correct number each time the clock strikes another hour. When the clock strikes one, shake one time; when the clock strikes two, shake two times, and so on.

Barner, Bob. *Parade Day: Marching Through the Calendar Year.*

2003. New York: Holiday House.

Summary: Reasons to have a parade are given for each month of the year.

Action: Find some great marching music and have it ready to play (John Philip Sousa composed many famous marches). Have the children stand up and form a circle before you start reading. Read the first page, then start the music and start marching in your circle. After about ten seconds, stop the music, stop the marching, and read the second page. Repeat marching to the music after each page.

Beaumont, Karen. *Baby Danced the Polka.*

2004. Illus., Jennifer Plecas. New York: Dial Books for Young Readers.

Summary: A baby dances instead of taking a nap.

Action: Have some music ready before you start to read the book. When you get to the first page where the baby dances, read the page, then turn on the music and dance with the kids. After about 20–30 seconds, turn the music off and have the kids stop dancing so you can read the next page (you may want them to sit back down to get them to stop dancing). Read until the next page where the baby dances and turn on the music again. Repeat for each dancing page. You can use polka music or any music that you like.

Bee, William. *And the Train Goes . . .*

2007. Cambridge, MA: Candlewick Press.

Summary: A train and the people aboard make many noises on a journey from one station to the next.

Action: There are many different noises in this book. One of them is repeated five times throughout the book: "and the train goes, Clickerty-click, clickerty-clack." Hand out shakers to the kids before you read the story. Practice shaking them whenever you say the repeated phrase. As you read the story aloud, have the kids shake their shakers along with the book.

Blackstone, Stella. *Who are you, Baby Kangaroo?*

2004. Illus., Clare Beaton. Cambridge, MA: Barefoot Books.

Summary: A puppy asks animals from around the world the name of a baby kangaroo.

Action: There is a repetitive phrase on each page of this book: "[animal], [animal], can you give me a clue? Can you tell me the name of the baby kangaroo?" This phrase can be said to the same beat each time, for example: "WOLF cubs, WOLF cubs, can you GIVE me a CLUE? Can you TELL me the NAME of the BAby kangaROO?" The capital letters signify the downbeats of the phrase; shake the shakers then. Give the children shakers and have them help you with this phrasing.

Butler, John. *Bedtime in the Jungle.*

2009. Atlanta: Peachtree.

Summary: Animals settle their children one to ten as nighttime comes in the jungle.

Action: Give each child a shaker before you start reading. Use the shakers to count out the number of babies on each page. For example, after you read "It was bedtime in the jungle, and the day was almost done. A rhino lay down quietly next to her baby one," shake your shakers one time. After you read "It was bedtime in the jungle, and the stream was shining blue. A monkey made a bed for her babies two," shake your shakers two times. Continue for each animal.

Calmenson, Stephanie. *Jazzmatazz!*

2008. Illus., Bruce Degen. New York: HarperCollins.

Summary: A mouse sneaks in and starts playing jazz. Soon everyone is joining in the music.

Action: Locate some instrumental jazz music in your collection. Play 10–15 seconds of music after every time you read "Doo-dat, diddy-dat, Diddy-dat, doo!" Let the kids dance to the music or give them instruments to play along.

Cohan, George M. *You're a Grand Old Flag: A Jubilant Song about Old Glory.*

2003. Illus., Todd Ouren. Minneapolis, MN: Picture Window Books.

——. *You're a Grand Old Flag.*

2007. Illus., Warren Kimble. New York: Walker.

Summary: Illustrated versions of the patriotic song.

Action: Give the children instruments and ask them to stand up. As you read and sing the song, have them march and play their instruments to the beat. If you are uncomfortable singing, find a recording of the song to play while you turn the pages.

Cox, Judy. *My Family Plays Music.*

2003. Illus., Elbrite Brown. New York: Holiday House.

Summary: A young girl tells about all the musical people in her family.

Action: Give each child an instrument to play. At the end of each page, have them play their instruments. For example, on the page that reads, "This is my mom. . . . When I play with her, I play the tambourine," after the last line ask the kids to play their instruments.

alternate activity
If you have all of the instruments in this book (tambourine, triangle, cymbals, cowbell, woodblock, maracas, jug, rhythm sticks, handbell, wind chimes, and soup kettle), give each to a child to play on the correct page.

Doyle, Malachy. *The Dancing Tiger.*

2005. Illus., Steve Johnson and Lou Fancher. New York: Viking.

Summary: A child dances with a tiger each time the moon is full.

Action: Play 10–20 seconds of music in between each set of pages so that everyone can dance with the tiger. You can make this book even more interactive by giving each child a die-cut tiger shape to dance with. Or if you have a tiger stuffed animal, the kids can take turns dancing with it.

Durango, Julia. *Cha-Cha Chimps.*

2006. Illus., Eleanor Taylor. New York: Simon and Schuster Books for Young Readers.

> **Summary:** Ten little chimps dance with other animals at Mambo Jamba's.

> **Action:** Most of the pages in this book end with the words "ee-ee-oo-oo-ah-ah-ah! 10 little chimps do the cha-cha-cha." The only difference is that the number of chimps decreases by one on each consecutive page. Play music for 10–20 seconds at the end of each page so everyone can dance with the chimps. You can decide whether or not to play music on the few pages where the chimps don't dance. For extra authenticity, play cha-cha music. If you have puppets or pictures for each of the animals (rhino, cobra, lion, cheetah, hippo, giraffe, meerkat, zebra, and ostrich), include them in the dancing fun either by holding them yourself or giving them to the kids to dance with.

Emberley, Rebecca. *There Was an Old Monster!*

2009. Illus., Rebecca Emberley and Ed Emberley. New York: Orchard Books.

> **Summary:** A version of "There Was an Old Lady Who Swallowed a Fly" with a monster that eats crazy animals.

> **Action:** Give each child an egg shaker or maraca. After the monster eats the ants, he dances in his pants "Scritchy-scratch, scritch, scritchy-scratch." That rhythm of words appears six times in the book. Each time you read it, dance with the kids while shaking the instruments to the rhythm.

Emmett, Jonathan. *She'll Be Coming 'Round the Mountain.*

2006. Illus., Deborah Allwright. New York: Atheneum Books for Young Readers.

> **Summary:** The classic song with brand-new verses.

> **Action:** Have the kids act out the motions for each of the verses as they sing along with the book. The last two pages give ideas for motions for each verse.

Gershator, Phillis, adapt. *This is the Day!*

2007. Illus., Marjorie Priceman. Boston: Houghton Mifflin.

> **Summary:** Many babies find homes in this song about the day we gave the babies away.

> **Action:** Give each child jingle bells. At the end of each verse are the words "tra la and fiddle de dee." Have everyone sing those words and shake the bells to the beat. You can use the musical score in the book or create your own rhythm.

Griessman, Annette. *Like a Hundred Drums.*

2006. Illus., Julie Monks. Boston: Houghton Mifflin.

Summary: A thunderstorm slowly creeps up on a summer day and everyone relaxes after it passes.

Action: Give every child a pair of rhythm sticks at the beginning of the book. After each page, have the kids knock their sticks together to simulate the slowly approaching thunder. Start off slow and quiet and increase with intensity as the storm gets closer. When the storm finally hits, have the kids knock their sticks together hard and fast. When the storm is done, have the kids put their sticks on the floor as you finish the rest of the story.

Hanson, Warren. *Bugtown Boogie.*

2008. Illus., Steve Johnson and Lou Fancher. New York: Laura Geringer Books.

Summary: A little boy finds bugs of all shapes and sizes dancing behind a magic door.

Action: The words "The Bugtown Boogie, shakin' up the woods tonight" appear seven times in the text. Whenever you read those words, turn on some music and let the kids dance for a few seconds before reading on.

Harby, Melanie. *All Aboard for Dreamland!*

2007. Illus., Geraldo Valerio. New York: Simon and Schuster Books for Young Readers.

Summary: Children take an imaginative train ride to dreamland.

Action: Give each child two shakers at the beginning of the book. Have them hold one shaker in each hand, bend their arms, and shake as they move like the wheels on a train. You can do the motions at the end of each page or whenever the train goes "clickety-clack." If you use the shakers after ever page, try to shake quieter as the story progresses toward dreamland.

Horáček, Petr. *Look Out, Suzy Goose.*

2008. Cambridge, MA: Candlewick Press.

Summary: Suzy Goose goes into the forest to be alone and barely escapes from a fox, wolf, and bear.

Action: Hand out four different types of musical instruments to the kids (bells, shakers, rhythm sticks, drums, maracas, etc.). When Suzy Goose goes flip flop into the forest, have the kids with bells shake their instruments. When the hungry fox tiptoes after Suzy, have the kids with the shakers use their instruments, then have the bells join in. When the wolf creeps after the fox and Suzy, have the kids with the rhythm sticks hit their instruments together, and then have the shakers and bells join in. Finally, when the bear pads after the wolf, fox, and Suzy, have the kids with the drums hit their instruments, and then have the rhythm sticks, shakers, and bells join in. When everybody runs from the owl, have all of the kids play their instruments loudly.

Hudson, Cheryl Willis. *My Friend Maya Loves to Dance.*

2010. Illus., Eric Velasquez. New York: Abrams Books for Young Readers.

Summary: Maya likes to dance to all sorts of music whenever she can.

Action: Create a playlist, CD, or cassette with short snippets (20–30 seconds) of the different types of music that Maya dances to. Play the corresponding music after you read each page of the book and let the children dance for a few seconds. A majority of the music will be ballet. You will also need tap, jazz, blues, rap, gospel, African, music by Bach, and reggae.

Isadora, Rachel. *Bring On That Beat.*

2002. New York: G. P. Putnam's Sons.

Summary: Jazz music brings everyone to life in the city.

Action: Find some instrumental jazz music with a good beat. A search for swing jazz is a good place to start in your library catalog. Start the music and start a clapping rhythm that the kids can follow. Then start reading this rhythmic story to the beat.

Jeffers, Oliver. *How to Catch a Star.*

2004. New York: Philomel Books.

Summary: A little boy is determined to catch a star to be his friend.

Action: The boy goes out early in the morning to try to find a star. He waits and waits and finally sees one just as the sun is about to set. When you get to that page, take a break from reading to sing "Twinkle, Twinkle, Little Star" as a group.

Johnson, Angela. *Violet's Music.*

2004. Illus., Laura Huliska-Beith. New York: Dial Books for Young Readers.

Summary: Violet loves music and finally finds some friends who like it, too.

Action: Many different types of instruments are referred to in this text. Locate a short snippet of music featuring each instrument. You will need to find: a rattle (or just shake a real rattle), a horn, a guitar, a drum, a saxophone, and someone singing. Whenever that instrument is mentioned in the text, play a few seconds of music featuring that instrument and have the kids pretend to play.

Karas, G. Brian. *Atlantic.*

2002. New York: G. P. Putnam's Sons.

Summary: Lyrical text celebrates the Atlantic Ocean.

Action: Many white noise machines have a setting for crashing waves. Play this in the background as you read the story. Have the kids put their hands together in front of them and swim/dance around like fish throughout the book.

Klinting, Lars. *What Do You Want?*

2006. Toronto: Groundwood Books.

Summary: Familiar objects and their partners are illustrated on back-to-back pages.

Action: Give each child a musical instrument. The best instrument to use is a drum; however, any instrument will do. Read the first page "The rooster wants . . ." and have the children play their instruments like a drumroll. Then flip the page to read what the rooster wants. Continue playing the instruments with each object throughout the book.

Kutner, Merrily. *Down on the Farm.*

2004. Illus., Will Hillenbrand. New York: Holiday House.

Summary: A mischievous goat travels through his farm.

Action: The words "Down on the farm" appear twice on each page. Give the children shakers that they can shake to the rhythm of those words on each page. On the last page, have them shake the shakers very quietly as the farm goes to sleep.

Lewis, Kevin. *Tugga-Tugga Tugboat.*

2006. Illus., Daniel Kirk. New York: Hyperion Books for Children.

Summary: A hardworking tugboat has lots of duties during the day.

Action: Give the children instruments of your choice (rhythm sticks, bells, shakers) and have them follow the rhythm of the text with their instruments. The words "Tugga-tugga tugboat" appear five times in the text.

Those words and the line after them have a good rhythm, for example, "TUGga-TUGga TUGboat, BOUNCE and BOB and FLOAT, boat" (use the instruments on the syllables with all capital letters).

London, Jonathan. *Froggy Plays in the Band.*

2002. Illus., Frank Remkiewicz. New York: Viking.

Summary: Froggy and his friends start a marching band to compete in the contest.

Action: Once Froggy starts his band with his friends, give every child an instrument. It is best if you use a variety of instruments. Starting on that page, have the children march and play their instruments in order to help Froggy and his friends practice and compete. March and play the instruments for a few seconds at the end of each page.

Macken, JoAnn Early. *Sing-Along Song.*

2004. Illus., LeUyen Pham. New York: Viking.

Summary: A young boy is inspired to sing all day long.

Action: Have everyone stand up at the beginning of the book. Whenever the young boy sings, create a rhythm and sing along with him. Everyone else can dance with your singing. If you don't like singing in front of a crowd, you can play music in the background as you read what the boy sings.

Manning, Maurie J. *The Aunts Go Marching.*

2003. Honesdale, PA: Boyds Mills Press.

Summary: A little girl and her drum draw many aunts to the street to march to town.

Action: Give each child a pair of rhythm sticks. Have them march in place to the story. At the end of each verse are the words "Rat a tat-tat! Rat a tat-tat! Ba-rump, ba-rump, ba-rump!" Have the children beat their rhythm sticks together whenever you read those words.

———. *Kitchen Dance.*

2008. New York: Clarion Books.

Summary: Two children sneak out of bed to watch their parents dance in the kitchen.

Action: At the point in the story when the father and mother catch the children watching them, turn on some music and have everyone dance for about 30 seconds.

McCarthy, Mary. *A Closer Look.*

2007. New York: Greenwillow Books.

Summary: An image of a bug, flower, and bird are shown up close and then zoomed out so the whole object can be seen.

Action: Give each child an instrument. Each of the three images is built up with suspense over four pages. At the end of each suspense page ("Look!" "What do you . . ." and "See?"), have the kids play their instruments like a drumroll.

Mitton, Tony. *Dinosaurumpus!*

2002. Illus., Guy Parker-Rees. New York: Orchard Books.

Summary: All the dinosaurs gather together to dance.

Action: Give each child an egg shaker or maraca or other instrument that makes a shaker sound. The following stanza is repeated nine times in the text: "Shake, shake, shudder . . . near the sludgy old swamp. The dinosaurs are coming. Get ready to romp." (Halfway through the book, the stanza changes to "Everybody's doing the dinosaur romp.") Have everyone dance and shake their instruments to the beat of those words.

Moss, Lloyd. *Our Marching Band.*

2001. Illus., Diana Cain Bluthenthal. New York: G. P. Putnam's Sons.

Summary: Ten neighborhood kids learn to play instruments and create a marching band.

Action: On the day when the kids are finally ready to make their parade debut, give every child a musical instrument. There are five page spreads where the kids are marching in the parade. Play marching music (John Philip Sousa composed some nice choices) for a few seconds at the end of each of these pages. Have the kids march in a circle playing their instruments along with the music.

———. *Music Is.*

2003. Illus., Philippe Petit-Roulet. New York: G. P. Putnam's Sons.

Summary: A description of the many ways to enjoy music and how it makes people feel.

Action: Give every child a musical instrument at the beginning of the book. You can use all the same instruments or a variety of different ones. At the end of every page, have the children play their instruments for a few seconds. For added movement, you can have everyone march around the room when the book refers to marching bands.

Peters, Andrew Fusek. *Animals Aboard!*

2007. Illus., Jim Coplestone. London: Frances Lincoln Children's Books.

Summary: Animals jump aboard a train and have a party with music before they all fall asleep.

Action: Give each child a musical instrument and a die-cut shape of a cow, duck, horse, pig, hen, or cat. If you don't have die-cut shapes for all of the animals, you can use photocopied images of each animal. When the cow jumps on the train, have all of the kids with cow shapes hold up their shapes. Do the same as each animal joins the train. When the cow plays music on the train, have all of the kids with cow shapes play their instruments. Again, do the same as each animal joins in the music. Finally, at the end of the story when all of the animals are asleep, have all the kids put their animal shapes on the floor so they can sleep, too.

Pritchett, Dylan. *The First Music.*

2006. Illus., Erin Bennett Banks. Little Rock, AR: August House.

Summary: African animals create a unique rhythm and music.

Action: Give everyone a shaker. The first sound that is made by the animal is "padada pada-pada." Whenever you say those words, have the kids shake their shakers. When the elephants join in, they make a "boom" sound by beating on a log. Have the children stomp their feet whenever you say "boom." These two sounds are intertwined throughout the story.

Protopopescu, Orel. *Two Sticks.*

2007. Illus., Anne Wilsdorf. New York: Farrar Straus and Giroux.

Summary: When Maybelle's sticks cause a ruckus and charm a group of crocodiles, her parents finally decide to buy her a drum.

Action: Give everyone two rhythm sticks. The word *sticks* appears 23 times in the text. Every time you read that word, have everyone clap their sticks together. Or, they can tap out a beat at the end of every page with the sticks.

Rosenthal, Amy Krouse. *Yes Day!*

2009. Illus., Tom Lichtenheld. New York: HarperCollins.

Summary: On Yes Day, a little boy gets everything he asks for.

Action: Give everyone an instrument. Whenever the boy asks for something on this special day, the answer is yes. After you read each question, have the children play their instruments loudly and say "YES!" For example, "Can I please have pizza for breakfast?" The children can shake their bells and say "YES!" The instruments add another fun level to this special day in a little boy's life.

Shannon, David. *Duck on a Bike.*

2002. New York: The Blue Sky Press.

> **Summary:** When the other farm animals see Duck riding a bike, they all decide to join in the fun.

> **Action:** Give every child a set of jingle bells. If possible, bring in a bicycle bell. Ring the bell for the kids and explain what it is. Tell them that they all have their own bells to use as bicycle bells. As Duck rides the bike, he passes many different farm animals. Each time, he says "Hello" and rides on. Whenever Duck says "Hello" to another farm animal, the children can shake their bicycle bells (jingle bells). When you get to the page where all of the animals are riding bikes, have the children shake their bells loudly to imitate a whole bunch of bicycle bells.

Smee, Nicola. *Clip-Clop.*

2006. New York: Boxer Books.

> **Summary:** Cat, Dog, Pig, and Duck all go for a fun and fast ride on Mr. Horse's back.

> **Action:** Give every child two rhythm sticks. When Mr. Horse runs with the other animals on his back, he goes "Clip-clop, clippity-clop." Whenever you read those words, have the children hit two rhythm sticks together. They can hit the sticks together faster when the animals request a faster ride.

Stutson, Caroline. *Cats' Night Out.*

2010. Illus., J. Klassen. New York: Simon and Schuster Books for Young Readers.

> **Summary:** Cats dance the night away on city streets and rooftops.

> **Action:** Have music ready to play before you start reading the book. Any kind of music will work for this activity. At first there are two cats dancing. Ask for two volunteers to come to the front of the room to dance. Play a few seconds of music while they dance. Then there are four cats dancing. Ask for two more volunteers to dance and play a few seconds of music. More and more cats join in pairs of two. Keep asking for more and more kids to join the dance until you have twenty kids (cats) just like the book. If there are more kids in your program, ask everyone to join

the dance before the neighbors stop the fun. At that point, ask everyone to sit back down while you finish the last couple pages of the book.

Walton, Rick. *How Can You Dance?*

2001. Illus., Ana López-Escrivá. New York: G. P. Putnam's Sons.

Summary: Children dance imaginatively like different animals and other things in their lives.

Action: Have some fun kids' music ready to play before you start reading the story. It doesn't matter what you play; just find something that you like. At the end of each page, play a little music and encourage the kids to dance like the book:

- Bounce like a kangaroo—Dance by jumping around.
- When one foot is sore—Dance by hopping.
- Like a frog—Dance by pretending to swim like a frog.
- Like a tree—Dance by waving your arms in the air like the branches of a tree.
- Like you're the king of the cha-cha-cha—Dance by just moving your feet.
- Like a crab—Dance by stepping from side to side.
- Like a fox—Dance by running quickly in place.
- Like the leader of a band—Dance by marching.
- Like a bee—Dance by holding your finger out and flying it around the room like a bee.
- Like a donkey carrying a pack—Dance by bending at your waist and moving slowly.
- Like a snake—Dance by slithering on the floor or by holding your arms at your side and wiggling around.
- Like a cloud—Dance by waving good-bye as you slowly walk away.

Webb, Steve. *Tanka Tanka Skunk!*

2003. New York: Orchard Books.

Summary: Rhythm is found in the syllables of animal names.

Action: Give every child a musical instrument to play. Shakers and rhythm sticks work especially well with this book. If you don't have musical instruments, the kids can hit the floor like a drum. The phrase "Skunka Tanka Skunka Tanka Tanka Tanka Skunk!" appears five times in the text.

Whenever you read those words, have the kids play the instruments to the beat of the words. To make things more interesting, they can play the instruments to the beat of all the animals in the book. If you choose to do this, it is recommended that you read each page once, and then read it a second time with the instruments so that the kids have already heard the beat of the page.

Wheeler, Lisa. *Jazz Baby.*

2007. Illus., R. Gregory Christie. Orlando: Harcourt.

Summary: The whole family joins together to make some jazz music.

Action: Give every child a musical instrument. The baby joins in the fun on almost every page. Whenever the baby adds to the music, have the children play their instruments.

Wilson, Karma. *Hilda Must Be Dancing.*

2004. Illus., Suzanne Watts. New York: Margaret K. McElderry Books.

Summary: Whenever Hilda dances, she makes so much noise that the other animals try to help her find another hobby.

Action: Have some music ready to play before you start reading the book. Any type of music will work for this story. Whenever Hilda starts dancing and making lots of noise, turn on the music and dance with everyone for a few seconds. Then stop the music and continue reading until Hilda dances again.

tip The motions for "Twinkle, Twinkle, Little Star" are simple. Have the children close both of their hands into a fist and then spread them wide to imitate a twinkling star. Do this motion to the beat of the song. Encourage the children to raise their hands above their heads and continue "twinkling" for the words "Up above the world so high like a diamond in the sky."

Wilson-Max, Ken. *Max's Starry Night.*

2001. New York: Hyperion Books for Children.

Summary: Max's friend, Big Blue, is scared of the dark, so Max finds a way for them to enjoy the stars while safe inside their house.

Action: When Max convinces Big Blue to come outside to see the stars, the three friends sing "Twinkle, Twinkle, Little Star." At that point in the story, stop reading so everyone can sing the song and do the motions together. Although it is not part of the story, sing the song again when Max shows Big Blue and Little Pink that he has hung stars from his ceiling.

Winthrop, Elizabeth. *Dumpy La Rue.*

2001. Illus., Betsy Lewin. New York: Henry Holt.

Summary: Dumpy likes to dance even though his family thinks it is strange. Eventually everyone at the farm joins in the fun.

Action: Dumpy La Rue dances all by himself for the first part of the book. When all of the other animals decide to join in, stop reading for a little while and play some music so everyone in the program can dance with Dumpy.

Wong, Janet S. *Buzz.*

2000. Illus., Margaret Chodos-Irvine. San Diego: Harcourt.

Summary: While a young boy's parents get ready in the morning, he observes many things that buzz like a bee.

Action: Give everyone an egg shaker or other instrument. Whenever the child observes something making a buzzing sound, have the children shake their instruments to make noise.

Yolen, Jane, and Heidi E. Y. Stemple. *Not All Princesses Dress in Pink.*

2010. Illus., Anne-Sophie Lanquetin. New York: Simon and Schuster Books for Young Readers.

Summary: Princesses come in all shapes and sizes and do lots of "nonprincess" activities.

Action: Each of the princesses in this book wears a "sparkly crown." Give every child a set of jingle bells to ring every time you say "sparkly crown."

playacting

Swim like a fish and fly like an airplane! The characters in picture books always have the best adventures. By following the clear directions in this chapter, the children in your program can pretend along with the book. Point at a spot on the floor and tell your audience that a baby chick is stuck in the mud. They will gladly help to "pull" the chick to safety. When various vehicles are featured in a story, try to pretend that you are one of those vehicles. Don't be surprised to hear stories the next week about kids pretending to be tigers at the dinner table.

tips

- Ask the adults in the room to participate with their children.
- Whenever possible, model the movements for the children to follow.
- Some of these books suggest many different movements, sometimes many on the same page. Do the number of movements/motions that are comfortable for you and your audience.
- It is okay to take a few seconds to let the kids do (or figure out how to do) the movement before you continue reading. This will be helpful for books such as *This Jazz Man* and *Here We Go Round the Mulberry Bush*.

- Have a bell, whistle, or other noisemaker ready as a signal for movement to stop when reading books such as *April Foolishness*. Practice moving until the bell rings before you start reading the story.
- It is okay for the kids to be moving during an entire book such as *Sputter, Sputter, Sput!* Some of the kids will pay more attention to the story. Some may seem not to hear the story at all. They are all enjoying their personal interaction with the book (and are probably hearing more that you realize).
- During books such as *What We Do*, it will be easier to let the kids stand during the entire story rather than having them sit down in between each movement. Stand up while you read so that everyone can still see the book.
- When you are doing only one movement during a book, such as when you are reading *Big Scary Monster*, practice the movement with the group before you start reading.

Adams, Diane. *I Can Do It Myself!*

2009. Illus., Nancy Hayashi. Atlanta: Peachtree.

> **Summary:** Emily Pearl is a very big girl who can do things without Mom's help except when nighttime comes.
>
> **Action:** Instruct the children to act out Emily's actions on each page. For example:
>
> - "She can pour her own juice."—Pretend to pour juice into a cup.
> - "She can wash her own face."—Pretend to wash your face.
> - You may want to be careful with "She can blow her own nose." I suggest pretending to sneeze.

Aliki. *All by Myself!*

2000. New York: HarperCollins.

> **Summary:** A young boy goes through the school day by doing things all by himself.
>
> **Action:** Have the children act out as many actions as you want on each page. They can pretend to brush their teeth, pour milk on their cereal, paint a picture, practice playing the violin, and so forth.

Andreasen, Dan. *The Treasure Bath.*

2009. New York: Henry Holt.

> Summary: A young boy has an imaginative adventure in the bathtub.
>
> Action: Have the children act out the actions on each page of this book: mix the cake, put it in the oven, walk to the bathtub, take off your shirts (careful to make sure they pretend), play with your toy boats, swim with the fish, follow your maps, pry open the treasure chest, wash your hair, put on your pajamas, and eat some cake.

Axtell, David. *We're Going on a Lion Hunt.*

2000. New York: Henry Holt.

> Summary: Two children go through long grass, a lake, a swamp, and a big dark cave in search of a lion.
>
> Action: Instruct the kids to act out the long grass, lake, swamp, and dark cave:
>
> - For the long grass, walk as you push tall grass out of the way.
> - For the lake, pretend to flap your arms as if you are swimming.
> - For the swamp, walk like your feet keep getting stuck in the mud.
> - For the cave, hold out your flashlight and stoop down to walk.
> - Have them do the actions in reverse order after they find the lion.

Ayres, Katherine. *A Long Way.*

2003. Illus., Tricia Tusa. Cambridge, MA: Candlewick Press.

> Summary: A young girl takes a box to Grandma's while pretending that the box is different forms of transportation.
>
> Action: Tell the kids to act out the different forms of transportation that the box takes:
>
> - When it is a car, hold your hands in front of you like you are turning a steering wheel.
> - When it is a boat, stand unsteady like you are trying to find your sea legs.
> - When it is an airplane, put your arms straight out and "fly" around the room.
> - When it is a subway, hold onto the bar above you and sway with the movement of the train.
> - Finally, walk to Grandma's house.

Baicker, Karen. *I Can Do It Too!*

2003. Illus., Ken Wilson-Max. Brooklyn, NY: Handprint Books.

Summary: A little girl shows the world that she can do the same things her family can do.

Action: The little girl does lots of big-girl things in this story. Pretend to act out the actions with the kids in your storytime: pour juice, put on your clothes, mix cake batter, read a book, play a guitar, kiss an ouch good-bye, sip tea, ride a bicycle, and shout "Hooray!"

Bajaj, Varsha. *How Many Kisses Do You Want Tonight?*

2004. Illus., Ivan Bates. New York: Little, Brown.

Summary: Animals tuck their babies into bed with kisses from one to ten.

Action: The baby animals request different types of kisses in this book. Many of them request kisses on specific body parts: hair, beak, back, legs, and so forth. Whenever a body part is mentioned, ask the kids to touch that part of their own bodies.

Barroux, Stephane. *Where's Mary's Hat?*

2003. New York: Viking.

Summary: Mary asks many different hat-wearing animals if they have seen her hat.

Action: If you have a stuffed animal or puppet for each of the animals in the story, set them around the room. If not, create a picture of each of the animals to post around the room. Have the kids move around the room with you to ask if that animal has seen Mary's hat. Make sure that the bear has a hat kite.

Bateman, Teresa. *April Foolishness.*

2004. Illus., Nadine Bernard Westcott. Morton Grove, IL: Albert Whitman.

Summary: Two children try to trick their grandfather into believing that the farm animals have escaped on April Fools' Day.

Action: Have the kids act like each of the farm animals as they are mentioned in the book. For example, when "the cows have got loose," they can walk around the room on all fours and moo like cows.

Bauer, Marion Dane. *One Brown Bunny.*

2009. Illus., by Ivan Bates. New York: Orchard Books.

Summary: A lonesome bunny talks to many animals and objects as he tries to find a friend.

Action: Tell the kids to move like each of the animals/objects that the bunny talks to:

- Flap your arms and fly like the birds.
- Growl and walk away like the bears.
- Put your hands together to swim like a fish.
- Make yourself really small to be a mouse.
- Stand tall with your arms by your sides and sway to be a snake.
- Buzz around the room like a bee.
- Stand tall and still like a flower.
- Hold your arms out in a circle and move slowly to be a light and breezy cloud.
- Flap your wings and fly like a butterfly.

Bell, Babs. *Sputter, Sputter, Sput!*

2008. Illus., Bob Staake. New York: HarperCollins.

Summary: A boy rides in his car until it runs out of gas and he gets a fill-up.

Action: Have the children put their hands out like they are holding steering wheels and walk around like they are driving cars. They can drive uphill, downhill, up and down, and past houses. Have them stand still holding their steering wheels when the car in the story runs out of gas.

Bergman, Mara. *Yum Yum! What Fun!*

2009. Illus., Nick Maland. New York: Greenwillow Books.

Summary: Two children are too busy cooking to notice all of the animals sneaking into their house.

Action: Have the kids pretend to sneak into the house like each of the animals. Have them crawl on all fours and wag their tails like crocodiles, stomp their feet like camels, slither like snakes, gallop like horses, and put out their claws and crash in like bears.

Blake, Quentin. *Mrs. Armitage: Queen of the Road.*

2003. Atlanta: Peachtree.

Summary: Mrs. Armitage loses pieces of her vehicle while on a drive, but ends up with a cool machine.

Action: Mrs. Armitage loses hubcaps, fenders, bumpers, the hood, the roof, and the doors off her car. When she throws them into the trash, have the kids also pretend to throw them into the trash. They can also pretend to drive along with Mrs. Armitage.

Blake, Robert J. *Fledgling.*

2000. New York: Philomel Books.

Summary: A falcon takes its first flight in the city.

Action: Have the kids act like the fledgling and fly around the room as you read. They can set their feet, shake their wings, and jump into the air. Tell them to fly faster to escape the hawk. When the fledgling is lost, the children can put their hands above their eyes and look for home.

Bogan, Paulette. *Goodnight Lulu.*

2003. New York: Bloomsbury Children's Books.

Summary: Momma Chicken solves Lulu's nighttime fears.

Action: Have the children help Momma Chicken scare away the bear, tiger, and alligator:

- For the bear, flap your arms and cluck while you chase an imaginary bear.
- For the tiger, pull on an imaginary tiger tail and roar.
- For the alligator stomp and yell and chase.
- Finally, when the pigs come in, hug, squeeze, and kiss imaginary pigs.

Bonnett-Rampersaud, Louise. *How Do You Sleep?*

2005. Illus., Kristin Kest. Tarrytown, NY: Marshall Cavendish Children.

Summary: Rhyming text shows how six different animals (and humans) sleep.

Action: As you read about each animal, encourage the children to act out how the animal sleeps:

- Bird—Snuggle onto your nest and settle your wings back.
- Bear—Curl into a ball.
- Horse—Stand up and shut your eyes.
- Pig—Lay flat on your stomach with your hooves (arms) in front of you.
- Frog—Leap up onto your lily pad.
- Rabbit—Crawl underground and curl up.
- Children—Pull up your blanket and listen to a story.

Brett, Jan. *Honey . . . Honey . . . Lion!*

2005. New York: G. P. Putnam's Sons.

Summary: When honey badger gets greedy with the honey, Honeyguide leads honey badger on a trip he'll never forget.

Action: There are lots of great motions to act out with the kids in this book: zigzag over the baobab tree roots, splash across the water hole, bounce off the termite mound, stomp along a hollow log, push reeds out of the way, and swish through grass. Then do everything quickly in the reverse order as everyone runs from the lion.

Bruel, Robert O. *Bob and Otto.*

2007. Illus., Nick Bruel. New Milford, CT: Roaring Brook Press.

Summary: A caterpillar and a worm are best friends even when the caterpillar becomes a butterfly.

Action: Have the kids act out the movements of Bob and Otto. They can pretend to climb, eat, sleep, and fly with Bob. They can pretend to dig with Otto.

Cartwright, Reg. *What We Do.*

2004. New York: Henry Holt.

Summary: A variety of animals show how they wiggle, creep, swim, and so on.

Action: Instruct the kids to act like each animal as you read about it in the book:

- Wiggle—Wiggle your whole body.
- Creep—Crawl around on the floor.
- Swim—Put your hands together and wave them back and forth like a fish swimming.

- Leap—Leap in the air.
- Swing—Pretend to hold something with your hands as you swing around.
- Waddle—Put your hands down by your sides and waddle with your legs close together.
- Jump—Jump in the air.
- Paddle—Hold your hands out and paddle them like duck feet.
- Flutter—Wave your arms.
- Scurry—Hunch down to make yourself small and hurry around the room.
- March—March in place.
- Hop—Hop in the air.
- Dig—Pretend to dig in the ground.
- Fly—Flap your arms.
- Guzzle—Pretend to shovel food in your mouth.
- Climb—Pretend to climb something tall.
- Slide—Put your hands to your sides and sway back and forth.
- Wallow—Sit down and don't move.
- Glide—Pretend to swim very smoothly.
- Crawl—Crawl around on the floor.
- Bray—Bray like a donkey.
- Stretch—Stretch your neck very tall.
- Play—Act however you want.

Clarke, Jane. *Stuck in the Mud.*

2007. Illus., Garry Parsons. New York: Walker.

Summary: Many farm animals try to help Hen push and pull her chick out of the mud.

Action: You can have the kids participate in this story either standing up or sitting down. When each animal tries to push the stuck chick, have the children put their arms out and pretend to push on something. When each animal tries to pull the chick out, the children can put their hands together as if they are pulling on a rope and pretend to pull on something. If the kids are standing up, they can pretend that their feet are stuck as each new animal gets stuck in the mud.

Craig, Lindsey. *Dancing Feet!*

2010. Illus., Marc Brown. New York: Alfred A. Knopf.

Summary: Animals dance with their happy feet.

Action: Encourage the children to dance the way each animal dances in this book:

- Dance lightly with the "little black feet" of the ladybug.
- Dance hard with the "big gray feet" of the elephant.
- Dance like you have webbed feet with the "webbed orange feet" of the duck.
- Dance like you are creeping along with the "lots of purple feet" of the caterpillar.
- Dance loud with the "furry brown feet" of the bear.
- Dance like a tap dancer with the "long green feet" of the lizard.

Docherty, Thomas. *Big Scary Monster.*

2009. Somerville, MA: Templar Books.

Summary: A big scary monster learns that it is more fun to have friends than to scare all of the other animals.

Action: The word "Boo!" appears four times in this book. Each time it happens, have the children help you read it by jumping up and yelling "BOO!"

Ehrhardt, Karen. *This Jazz Man.*

2006. Illus., R. G. Roth. Orlando, FL: Harcourt.

Summary: A new version of "This Old Man" featuring famous musicians.

Action: Act out the motions of the musicians in this book, and encourage the children to imitate you:

- "This jazz man, he plays one"—Snap your fingers.
- "This jazz man, he plays two"—Dance with your feet.
- "This jazz man, he plays three"—Pretend your knees are drums.
- "This jazz man, he plays four"—Pretend to conduct an orchestra.
- "This jazz man, he plays five"—Pretend to play a saxophone.
- "This jazz man, he plays six"—Pretend to play the drums.
- "This jazz man, he plays seven"—Pretend to play a trumpet.

- "This jazz man, he plays eight"—Pretend to play a piano.
- "This jazz man, he plays nine"—Pretend to play a bass.

Fatus, Sophie, illus. *Here We Go Round the Mulberry Bush.*

2007. Cambridge, MA: Barefoot Books.

Summary: A new version of the classic song that shows children in four different countries getting ready for school.

Action: Teach the children to act out the motions for each verse of this song:

- "Here we go round the mulberry bush"—Turn in a circle in place.
- "This is the way we jump out of bed"—Jump in place.
- "This is the way we wash ourselves"—Pretend you have a wash-cloth as you wash parts of your body.
- "This is the way we brush our teeth"—Smile and use your finger as a toothbrush.
- "This is the way we comb our hair"—Run your fingers through your hair.
- "This is the way we put on our clothes"—Pretend to put on pants and a shirt.
- "This is the way we eat our food"—Pretend to put food in your mouth and chew.
- "This is the way we clean our bowls"—Cup one hand into a bowl shape and pretend to wash it out with the other hand.
- "This is the way we go to school"—Walk in place.
- "This is the way we wave good-bye"—Wave good-bye.

Fearnley, Jan. *Watch Out!*

2004. Cambridge, MA: Candlewick Press.

Summary: Wilf the mouse is too busy having fun to listen to his mother and ends up crashing and falling.

Action: Wilf (or his mother) falls with a "Crash Bang Wallop!" five times in this book (one fall is with a "Splish Splash Wallop!"). Have the kids act like Wilf and then fall to the ground with him: run in place, pretend to climb quickly, stir a pot of honey, and jump in mud. When his mother rushes for a cuddle, have the kids hold their arms and run in place again. After they fall to the ground each time, have them stand up while you read until you get to Wilf's next fun activity.

Feiffer, Jules. *The Daddy Mountain.*

2004. New York: Michael Di Capua Books.

Summary: A young girl slowly climbs up her father's body.

Action: The little girl climbs up parts of her father's body and clothing. She climbs using his feet, leg, knees, belt, shirt, collar, shoulder, ear, and head. As she climbs a particular part, have the kids touch that part of their own bodies or clothing.

Fleming, Denise. *The Cow Who Clucked.*

2006. New York: Henry Holt.

Summary: A cow wakes up one morning to find that she clucks instead of moos and go off to find her moo.

Action: Set up pictures or puppets of the animals that the cow talks to. You will need the following: dog, bee, cat, fish, duck, goat, mouse, snake, squirrel, owl, and hen. Put these animals around the room or storytime area. As you read the story, have the kids walk with you to the matching animal. After the cow says "Cluck, cluck," ask the kids what the new animal says before reading it out of the book. Then move on to the next animal.

Gay, Marie-Louise. *Roslyn Rutabaga and the Biggest Hole on Earth!*

2010. Toronto: Groundwood Books.

Summary: Roslyn tries to dig to the South Pole but keeps finding other animals in her way.

Action: Roslyn spends a lot of time digging in this book. Whenever she starts a new hole, have everyone pretend to dig for awhile.

Gorbachev, Valeri. *The Big Trip.*

2004. New York: Philomel Books.

Summary: Goat tells Pig about all the issues with traveling, unless you travel with a friend.

Action: Pig wants to travel and mentions many different methods of transportation. Act out each of the different types he mentions and have the kids follow along:

- Bike—Stand up, pretend to hold handlebars, and lift one knee at a time to peddle.

- Car—Hold your arms out as if holding a steering wheel.
- Horse—Gallop around the room.
- Donkey cart—Hold your arms out as if holding onto reins.
- Train—Bend your arms at your sides and move them in a circle like train wheels.
- Plane—Hold your arms out straight to pretend to fly.
- Hot-air balloon—Hold your arms up high and sway with the wind.
- Ship—Sway side to side with the waves.

Hayes, Sarah. *Dog Day.*

2008. Illus., Hannah Broadway. New York: Farrar Straus Giroux.

Summary: Ben and Ellie have a great day at school with their new teacher, who is a dog.

Action: In this story, the students all act like their dog teacher. Have the kids act along with the story: bark, wag your bottoms, scratch your ears, scratch under your chins, scratch all over, shake all over, sniff, pretend to dig a hole, stick out your tongues and pant, pretend to throw a ball, run to bring the ball back, lift your legs, lay down for a nap, sniff again, show your teeth, growl, and wag your bottoms again.

Heap, Sue. *What Shall We Play?*

2002. Cambridge, MA: Candlewick Press.

Summary: Three friends pretend to be many different things during their playtime.

Action: Have the kids join you in pretending along with Lily May, Matt, and Martha:

- Pretend to be trees—Put your hands up tall to be a big tree, shake your whole body to be a shaky tree, stand tall and quiet to be a quiet tree, and reach as high as you can to be trees in a row reaching for the sky.
- Pretend to be cars—Hold the steering wheel and run fast in place to be a fast car, hold the steering wheel and jump to be a bumpy car, pretend to honk the horn to be beep-beep cars in a traffic jam.
- Pretend to be cats—Crawl slowly to be a slow cat, lie down on the ground to be a sleepy cat, crawl stealthily to be a creeping cat, and meow and wash your cheek with your fist to be a noisy washing cat.

- Pretend to be Jell-O—Stand and shake like Jell-O.
- Pretend to be a fairy—Hold your magic wand and pretend to fly.

Henkes, Kevin. *Little White Rabbit.*
2011. New York: Greenwillow Books.

> **Summary:** A little white rabbit wonders about the many things around him on his adventure.

> **Action:** Act out the adventure of the white rabbit with the kids: Hop along through the grass; stand really tall and hop again; stand really still like a rock; flap your arms like a butterfly; and hop quickly away from the cat.

Horáček, Petr. *Silly Suzy Goose.*
2006. Cambridge, MA: Candlewick Press.

> **Summary:** Suzy Goose wants to be different from all the other geese, but realizes it is good to be part of a crowd when there is a lion around.

> **Action:** Suzy Goose tries to act like many different animals in this book. Help the kids pretend to be those animals, too:

- Flap your arms to act like a bat.
- Squawk loudly to act like a toucan.
- Smoothly slide to one side to act like a penguin.
- Stretch your neck tall to act like a giraffe.
- Flap your arms as if you are splashing in a pool to act like an elephant.
- Jump to act like a kangaroo.
- Run in place quickly to act like an ostrich.
- Move your arms as if you are swimming to act like a seal.
- Roar loudly to act like a lion.
- Do everything quickly and in reverse order when Suzy Goose rushes back to her friends.

Hort, Lenny. *The Seals on the Bus.*
2000. Illus., G. Brian Karas. New York: Henry Holt.

> **Summary:** An adaption of the classic "Wheels on the Bus" song with numerous wild animals.

> **Action:** Instruct the children to act like all of the animals on the bus:

- Seals—Hold your arms out straight and clap.

- Tiger—Hold your hands like claws and pretend to scratch at the air.
- Geese—Flap your arms like wings.
- Rabbits—Jump up and down.
- Monkeys—Scratch your hands on either side of your stomach.
- Vipers—Stand straight and sway side to side.
- Sheep—Crawl on all fours.
- Skunks—Hold your nose like something smells bad.
- People—Run in place and yell "Help!"

Hunter, Tom. *Build It Up and Knock It Down.*

2002. Illus., James Yang. New York: HarperFestival.

Summary: Two characters illustrate opposite actions.

Action: Have the children act out each of the opposite actions in this book:

- "Say hello and say good-bye"—Wave with one hand and then with the other.
- "Nodding yes and nodding no"—Shake your head yes and then no.
- "Sitting down and standing up"—You can either sit all the way on the floor or just pretend to sit down.
- "Put it on and take it off"—Pretend to take a hat on and off.
- "Build it up and knock it down"—Pretend to stack blocks and then wave your hands to pretend to knock them down.
- "Turn it on and turn it off"—Pretend to flip a light switch each time.
- "Jumping high and crouching low"—Jump and then bend your knees.
- "Upside down and right-side up"—Bend at your waist until you are looking upside down and then stand up straight.
- "In and out"—Step forward to go in and then backward to go out.
- "Go away and come on back"—Wave your hand hello/good-bye as you step forward and back.

Johnson, Paul Brett. *On Top of Spaghetti.*

2006. New York: Scholastic Press.

Summary: An extension of the classic children's song.

Action: The restaurant owner recounts his tale of the runaway meatball many times throughout the story. Whenever you read/sing "When somebody sneezed," have everyone pretend to sneeze.

Kulka, Joe. *Wolf's Coming!*

2007. Minneapolis: Carolrhoda Books.

Summary: The animals all run from wolf in order to reach the house before him for his surprise party.

Action: For the first half of this book, the animals are running away quickly. Have everyone run in place along with the book. When you get to the page that says "Hush now, hush now. Not a peep. You must be still, like you're asleep," have everyone stand really still. When the "surprise" ending comes, have everyone yell "Surprise!" to the wolf.

Lawrence, John. *This Little Chick.*

2002. Cambridge, MA: Candlewick Press.

Summary: A little chick makes the sounds of other animals when it plays with them.

Action: Instruct the children to act out the way the chick interacts with the other animals in this book:

- Oink and jump and twirl around when the chick plays with the pigs.
- Quack and pretend to swim with the ducks.
- Moo and lie down with the cows.
- Ribbit and jump with the frogs.
- Baa and skip with the lambs.

Lewis, Kevin. *My Truck is Stuck!*

2002. Illus., Daniel Kirk. New York: Hyperion Books for Children.

Summary: A truck full of dog bones gets stuck in a hole and gets help from many other vehicles to get unstuck.

Action: A car, moving truck, jeep, school bus, and tow truck all help the stuck truck. Each time a vehicle tries to help, they "tug and tow." Whenever a vehicle is trying to pull the truck out of the hole, have everyone pull on an imaginary rope attached to the stuck truck. Also, as each vehicle approaches the stuck truck, they honk their horns. Have the children "beep beep" on their imaginary horns along with the book.

————. *Dinosaur Dinosaur.*

2006. Illus., Daniel Kirk. New York: Orchard Books.

Summary: A life in the day of a young dinosaur.

Action: Teach the kids to act out a number of the actions of the young dinosaur in this book:

- "wake up with a roar!"—Stretch and roar out loud.
- "stomp across the floor!"—Stomp your feet.
- "sit right down to eat"—Pretend to eat breakfast cereal.
- "all those teeth to brush" —Pretend to brush your teeth.
- "where's your other shoe?"—Look around the room as if you are looking for something.
- "run outside and play"—Run in place.
- "hopping everywhere!"—Hop on one foot.
- "bouncy-pouncy dinosaur"—Bounce up and down.
- "come and dine with me"—Pretend to eat spaghetti.
- "soap up in the tub"—Pretend to use a washcloth to take a bath.
- "stumble up the stairs"—Pretend to walk up stairs.
- "good night, sweet dreams"—Lay your head on your hands and close your eyes.

Lewis, Kim. *Good Night, Harry.*

2003. Cambridge, MA: Candlewick Press.

Summary: Harry tries to find a way to fall asleep.

Action: Have the kids act out some of the actions with Harry as he tries to fall asleep: pretend to hang up clothes, pretend to pick things off the floor to clean up the room, run in place, touch your toes, hop on one foot, jump up and down, stretch one way, stretch the other way, wiggle and squiggle and roll into a ball, and, finally, close your eyes and go to sleep.

Lord, Janet. *Where Is Catkin?*

2010. Illus., Julie Paschkis. Atlanta: Peachtree.

Summary: Catkin chases after many animals, ends up in a tall branch of a tree, and needs help getting down.

Action: Have everyone chase after the animals with Catkin: hop after the cricket, leap after the frog, jump after the mouse, race after the snake, and pounce after the bird.

Luthardt, Kevin. *Flying!*

2009. Atlanta: Peachtree.

> **Summary:** A little boy fantasizes about flying and pretends to with his father.
>
> **Action:** The little boy fantasizes about flying and then his father holds him up in the air so he can pretend to fly. Whenever the boy "flies," have the children hold out their arms and pretend to fly with him.

Martin, David. *We've All Got Bellybuttons!*

2005. Illus., Randy Cecil. Cambridge, MA: Candlewick Press.

> **Summary:** Animals have ears, hands, necks, feet, eyes, mouths, and belly buttons just like us.
>
> **Action:** For each of the body parts identified in the book, have everyone point to that area of their own bodies and then do the action associated with it:
>
> - Ears—Pull on your ears.
> - Hands—Clap your hands.
> - Necks—Stretch your neck really tall.
> - Feet—Kick your feet.
> - Eyes—Close your eyes.
> - Mouth—Open your mouth wide.
> - Belly button—Tickle your belly.

Masurel, Claire. *Domino.*

2007. Illus., David Walker. Cambridge, MA: Candlewick Press.

> **Summary:** Domino may be smaller than the other puppies, but he can still save the day.
>
> **Action:** Have the children act out movements with Domino and his friends: jump, run (in place), bark, jump again, run again, bark again, and pretend to crawl under a fence to retrieve the ball.

Mayhew, James. *Where's My Hug?*

2008. Illus., Sue Hellard. New York: Bloomsbury Children's Books.

> **Summary:** Jake's hug gets passed from person to person until he finally finds it.
>
> **Action:** Jake's hug gets passed to his father, the cat, a witch, a wizard, a knight, a princess, and a dragon. Each time the hug gets passed on, have

the children wrap their arms around their bodies for a hug or pretend to hug the person or animal receiving the hug.

Mayo, Margaret. *Dig Dig Digging.*

2001. Illus., Alex Ayliffe. New York: Henry Holt.

Summary: Various working vehicles show what they do all day.

Action: Encourage the children to pretend to be the many vehicles in this book:

- Diggers—Act like you are digging into the ground.
- Fire engines—Pretend to hold a hose and aim it at the fire.
- Tractors—Pretend to pull farm equipment behind you.
- Garbage trucks—Pretend to gobble up garbage.
- Cranes—Pretend to lift something heavy.
- Transporters—Hold out your arms as if you are carrying something and walk around the room.
- Dump trucks—Lean to the side as if you are pouring something out of your truck bed (may resemble "I'm a Little Teapot" pouring out tea).
- Rescue helicopters—Twirl your arms above your head like the blades of a helicopter.
- Road rollers—Roll your arms like the "Wheels on the Bus" song.
- Bulldozers—Pretend to push something heavy out of your way.
- Trucks—Hold out your arms to hold a steering wheel and pull your loud horn.

McClements, George. *Night of the Veggie Monster.*

2008. New York: Bloomsbury Children's Books.

Summary: A young boy turns into a monster every time he is forced to eat a vegetable.

Action: When the boy eats the pea, have the children pretend to turn into monsters with him:

- Wiggle your fingers.
- Rub your eyes as if they are watering.

- Move your feet all around as your toes twist and curl.
- Squirm in your seat.
- Finally, walk around the room like a great big monster.

McKenna, Sharon. *Good Morning, Sunshine: A Grandpa Story.*

2007. San Diego: Red Cygnet Press.

> **Summary:** Grandpa always knows how to make things right when his grand-daughter Katie gets a little grumpy.
>
> **Action:** Each time Katie gets grumpy, Grandpa helps her by saying good morning to the sunshine or good evening to the broccoli. Each time Katie and her grandpa say hello to something, have the kids throw their arms out and repeat after Katie and her grandpa: "Good morning sunshine," "Good morning clothes," "Good afternoon raindrops," "Good evening broccoli," and "Goodnight stars" (be sure to whisper the last one).

McMullan, Kate. *I'm Mighty!*

2003. Illus., Jim McMullan. New York: Joanna Cotler Books.

> **Summary:** A little tugboat helps larger boats get into the harbor.
>
> **Action:** The tugboat helps three very large boats get into port. Whenever he tugs the boats into safety, have the children pretend that they are tug-boats. They can pretend to pull and tug big huge boats through the water by acting like they are pulling a rope behind them.

Meister, Cari. *Tiny on the Farm.*

2008. Illus., Rich Davis. New York: Viking.

> **Summary:** A boy and his big dog, Tiny, help Uncle John find the missing kittens.
>
> **Action:** Eliot and Tiny look in the milk house, hayloft, horse stall, chicken coop, and shed for the kittens. Photocopy an image of these locations in the book, create a sign labeling the five locations, or simply pretend to go to the locations. Place the images or signs in different areas of your storytime space. When Eliot and Tiny look in each place, have every-one join you as you walk to the place and "search" for the kittens. Have stuffed animal kittens hidden in the shed to find along with Tiny.

Meyers, Susan. *This Is the Way a Baby Rides.*

2005. Illus., Hiroe Nakata. New York: Henry N. Abrams.

Summary: A comparison of human and animal babies and the things they do throughout the day.

Action: Show the children how to act out many of the movements that the babies make throughout their day:

- "This is the way a baby runs"—Run in place.
- "This is the way a baby hides"—Play peekaboo.
- "This is the way a baby jumps"—Jump in place.
- "This is the way a baby cries"—Hold your fists up to your eyes as you pretend to cry.
- "This is the way a baby eats"—Pretend to put food in your mouth and chew.
- "This is the way a baby flies"—Hold out your arms and fly around the room.
- "This is the way a baby swims"—Pretend to swim through water.
- "This is the way a baby plays"—Pretend to play tug-of-war.
- "This is the way a baby sleeps"—Put your hands together, close your eyes, and lay your head on your hands.
- "This is the way a baby wakes"—Stretch your arms high into the air.

Morrow, Tara Jaye. *Mommy Loves Her Baby/Daddy Loves His Baby*

2003. Illus., Tiphanie Beeke. New York: HarperCollins.

Summary: Mommy loves her baby as much as fish love the sea and kitties love to cuddle. Flip the book and Daddy loves his baby as much as bunnies love to bounce and bats love to sleep.

Action: You can choose to read one side of this flip book or both. Have the children pretend to act like the animals as you read about each one.

"Mommy" side of the book:
- "fishies love the seas"—Pretend to swim.
- "monkeys love bananas"—Pretend to peel and eat a banana.
- "squirrels love the trees"—Pretend to climb a tree.
- "penguins love to slide"—Hold your arms out in front of you and pretend to slide while standing up.
- "hyenas love to giggle"—Hold your sides and laugh out loud.
- "chameleons love to hide"—Play peekaboo.

- "lions love to roar"—Roar loudly.
- "beavers love to paddle"—Pretend that you have beaver arms and paddle through the water.
- "eagles love to soar"—Hold your arms out straight to each side and pretend to fly.
- "bear cubs love to rest"—Put your head down on your hands and close your eyes.
- "horsies love to gallop"—Gallop in place or around the room.
- "robins love to nest"—Pretend to settle down in a nest and wiggle your bottom as you get comfortable.
- "owls love to 'whooooo'"—Hoot like an owl.
- "turkeys love to gobble"—Gobble while shaking your hand under your chin like a turkey's wattle.
- "cows love to 'mooooo'"—Moo like a cow.
- "froggies love to leap"—Jump like a frog.
- "kitties love to cuddle"—Cuddle with a friend or family member in the group.
- "chickies love to 'peep'"—Peck at the ground with your hand while you peep.

"Daddy" side of the book:
- "leopards love to pounce"—Hold your hands like they are paws and pretend to leap onto your prey.
- "bumblebees love buzzing"—Hold out one finger and fly it around as you "buzz."
- "bunnies love to bounce"—Jump up and down.
- "puppies love to yap"—Bark like a dog.
- "giraffes love to stretch"—Stretch your neck really tall.
- "gators love to snap"—Hold one arm high and the other low and quickly clap your hands together like an alligator's mouth.
- "donkeys love to kick"—Kick with one leg.
- "camels love to carry"—Bend at your waist and pretend to carry something on your back.
- "llamas love to lick"—Stick out your tongue (but don't lick anything).
- "pandas love to chew"—Work your jaw like you are chewing on something.
- "roosters love to wake us with a 'cock-a-doodle-doo'"—Cock-a-doodle-doo like a rooster.

- "turtles love to creep"—Get low to the ground and creep around.
- "butterflies love flying"—Hold your arms like wings and flap them front and back.
- "bats love to sleep"—Bend at your waist so that your head is upside down and close your eyes.
- "gorillas love to swing"—Hold up one arm and pretend to swing on a vine.
- "cheetahs love to run"—Run quickly in place.
- "birdies love to sing"—Flap your arms and tweet like a bird.

Munsch, Robert. *Up, Up, Down.*

2001. Illus., Michael Martchenko. New York: Scholastic.

Summary: Anna likes to climb things, but often falls down. When she successfully climbs a tree, her mother and father fall trying to climb up to her.

Action: Whenever Anna or her parents climb something in this book, have everyone pretend to climb up something tall. Whenever they fall off of whatever they are climbing, have the children (carefully) fall on the floor as if they are singing "Ring Around the Rosy."

——. *More Pies!*

2002. Illus., Michael Martchenko. New York: Scholastic.

Summary: Samuel is so hungry that after eating a lot at home he still wins a pie-eating contest.

Action: The words "Chuka-chuka-chuka-chuka-chuka-chuka-CHOMP!" are repeated every time Samuel eats something in this book. Whenever you read those words, have the kids move their arms as if they are shoveling food into their mouths. Then have them open wide and close their mouths for "CHOMP!" These words are repeated seven times in the book.

Murphy, Mary. *Here Comes the Rain.*

2000. New York: Dorling Kindersley.

Summary: A cat tries to outrun a rain cloud but discovers that rain is really quite lovely.

Action: When the cat is trying to run away from the cloud, have everyone run in place. When the cat gets caught in the rain, have the kids pretend to make raindrops with their hands. To make raindrops, they can hold their arms out in front of them and wiggle their fingers while they lower their arms toward the ground.

O'Connell, Rebecca. *The Baby Goes Beep.*

2003. Illus., Ken Wilson-Max. Brookfield, CT: Roaring Brook Press.

Summary: A busy baby beeps, sings, eats, splashes, and sleeps.

Action: Do each of the motions with the baby as you read about them. For example: When "The baby goes Beep," pretend to honk a horn once. When "The baby goes Beep Beep," pretend to honk a horn twice. When "The Baby goes Beep Beep Beep Beep," pretend to honk a horn four times. Encourage the children to join you in using these motions for the rest of the book:

- "The baby goes Boom"—Pretend to play the drums on your legs.
- "The baby goes La"—Sing "La" with the baby.
- "The baby goes Flip"—Pretend to flip pages of a book.
- "The baby goes Yum"—Rub your stomach.
- "The baby goes Splash"—Flip your hands around as if you are splashing in water.
- "The baby goes Smooch"—Kiss into the air.
- "The baby goes Shhh"—Hold your finger up to your mouth and say "Shhh."

O'Connor, Jane. *Ready, Set, Skip!*

2007. Illus., Ann James. New York: Viking.

Summary: A little girl can do lots of cool things, but it takes a while for her to learn how to skip.

Action: Learn how to skip along with the girl in this book. When her mother asks her if she can hop, have everyone hop on one foot. Then practice hopping on one foot and then the other to skip in place.

Ormerod, Jan. *If You're Happy and You Know It!*

2003. Illus., Lindsey Gardiner. New York: Star Bright Books.

Summary: A twist on the classic children's song in which animals insist that they express happiness the best way.

Action: Have the children do all of the motions along with the girl and animals in this book:

- Clap your hands with the girl.
- Wave your tail with the dog—Shake your bottom.
- Flap your ears with the elephant—Hold your ears and flap them back and forth.

- Snap your teeth with the crocodile—Open your mouth wide and close it.
- Clack your beak with the toucan—Hold your hands up to your mouth like a beak and open and close them.
- Beat your chest with the gorilla—Tap your chest with your fists.
- Jump and bump with the kangaroo—Jump around.
- Screech with the parrot—Screech loudly.
- Laugh with the hyena—Hold your sides and laugh loudly.
- On the last page, do whatever makes you happy.

Parker, Marjorie Blain. *Mama's Little Duckling.*

2008. Illus., Mike Wohnoutka. New York: Dutton Children's Books.

Summary: Mama Quack and Dandelion Duckling save each other from different dangers near the water.

Action: Mama Quack warns Dandelion Duckling about the pike and the hawk by flapping her wings and quacking loudly. Dandelion Duckling does the same to warn Mama Quack about the weasel. When either duck warns the other duck, have the children flap their arms like wings and quack loudly.

Partridge, Elizabeth. *Whistling.*

2003. Illus., Anna Grossnickle Hines. New York: Greenwillow Books.

Summary: A young boy learns to whistle just in time to help the sun come up.

Action: Twice in this book the young boy tries too hard to whistle. At those two places in the book, ask everyone to take a deep breath and blow out hard. When the boy finally whistles, everyone can join him. Since whistling can be very hard for children (and some adults), kids can hum or make another noise when the boy whistles up the sun.

Patricelli, Leslie. *Higher! Higher!*

2009. Somerville, MA: Candlewick Press.

Summary: A little girl is pushed higher and higher on her swing until she swings up into space and meets an alien.

Action: When you start reading this book, have everyone move into a crouching position. As the little girl swings higher and higher, slowly start to stand up. When she swings up to the alien, everyone should be fully standing up. When she gives the alien a high five, have the children give someone standing near them a high five. Then have them slowly crouch back down again as the girl swings back toward Earth.

Paul, Ann Whitford. *If Animals Kissed Good Night.*
2008. Illus., David Walker. New York: Farrar, Straus and Giroux.

Summary: Rhyming text describes how animals kiss goodnight.

Action: For each animal described, instruct the children to kiss into the air and pretend to act like the animals:

- Sloth—Pretend to kiss very slowly.
- Peacock—Kiss while doing a dance.
- Python—Waggle and twist.
- Walrus—Pretend to tug on your whiskers.
- Elephant—Hold your arm/shoulder up to your chin like an elephant's trunk.
- Parrot—Hold your hand up to your mouth with your fingers pointing out and clack your fingers together like a beak.
- Wolf—Howl at the moon.
- Bear—Kiss and growl.
- Monkey—Hold one arm up in the arm and pretend to swing through the trees.
- Seal—Puff out your cheeks as if you are going to blow bubbles in water.
- Penguin—Pretend to hug a baby penguin.
- Rhino—Point one finger and hold it up to your face like a rhino horn.
- Giraffe—Stand very tall and stretch your neck out.
- Kangaroo—Jump around.
- Hippo—Wiggle your body slowly as you pretend to settle and get comfortable.

Pearson, Tracey Campbell. *Bob.*
2002. New York: Farrar Straus Giroux.

Summary: Bob the Rooster learns how to crow by asking other animals for help.

Action: Have the children take Bob's journey with him as he searches for his crow:

- When he learns how to "Meow," say "meow" together and pretend to tug on your whiskers.

- When he learns how to "Woof," say "woof" and wag your bottom (tail).
- When he learns how to "Ribbit," say "ribbit" and jump around like a frog.
- When he learns how to "Moo" and eat bugs, say "moo" and rub your stomach.
- When he finally learns how to "Cock-a-Doodle-Doo," say it with him and flap your arms like wings.
- As the story moves along, Bob adds each sound to the others. Be sure to do all of the motions whenever Bob meows, woofs, ribbits, moos, or cock-a-doodle-doos. Also, do everything loudly when Bob needs to scare the fox away.

Peck, Jan. *Way Up High in a Tall Green Tree.*

2005. Illus., Valeria Petrone. New York: Simon and Schuster Books for Young Readers.

> **Summary:** A little girl meets many animals as she climbs to the top of a tree before bedtime.
>
> **Action:** Have the children pretend to climb with the girl to the top of the tree. They can move their arms and legs as if they are climbing a ladder. After she greets each animal, she proceeds to "climb away." Everyone should keep climbing up until the last couple of pages where the girl climbs down to her waiting father.

Rex, Michael. *Dunk Skunk.*

2005. New York: G. P. Putnam's Sons.

> **Summary:** Animals play rhyming sports.
>
> **Action:** Have the kids follow along as you act out the sports actions of the animals:

- "Kick Chick"—Kick with one leg.
- "Goal Mole"—Hold your arms up as you pretend to block a soccer ball.
- "Bat Cat"—Hold a pretend baseball bat and swing it.
- "Glove Dove"—Pretend to catch a baseball or throw a softball into the group for someone to catch.

- "Freestyle Crocodile"—Hold your arms out and plant your feet side by side as you pretend to balance on a skateboard.
- "Lane Crane"—Hold your arm straight, swing it behind you, and then send a pretend bowling ball down the alley.
- "Dunk Skunk"—Hold one arm up in the air as you jump to make the basket.
- "Referee Kiwi"—Hold a pretend whistle in your hands near your mouth and whistle.
- "Putt Mutt"—Hold a pretend golf club and make the putt.
- "Coach Roach"—Bring everyone together into a huddle.
- "Quarterback Yak"—Hold a pretend football and throw it over your head.
- "Cheer Deer"—Jump up and down while waving pretend pom-poms.
- "Receiver Beaver"—Catch a pretend football or throw one into the group for someone to catch.
- "Hurdle Turtle"—Jump with your legs apart (one in front, one behind) as you pretend to hurdle.
- "Puck Duck"—Hold a pretend hockey stick and hit the puck.
- "Finish line Porcupine"—Hold your arms up in the air as you win the race.

Roep, Nanda. *Kisses.*

2002. Illus., Marijke ten Cate. Asheville, NC: Front Street.

Summary: Lisa's father offers many different kinds of kisses until she clarifies that she wants a goodnight kiss.

Action: Each page features the father offering a different kind of kiss. After reading each page, have everyone blow kisses into the air.

Root, Phyllis. *Looking for a Moose.*

2006. Illus., Randy Cecil. Cambridge, MA: Candlewick Press.

Summary: Four children go through woods, a swamp, some bushes, and up a hillside to find a moose.

Action: Go along with the children as they look for the moose:

- "Tromp Stomp" through the woods—Stomp your feet.
- "Squeech Squooch" through the swamp—Pretend to walk through deep mud.

- "Scritch Scratch" through the bushes—Push pretend branches out of your way as you walk in place.
- "Trip Trop" up the hillside—Take big steps as you pretend to walk over big boulders.

———. *Flip, Flap, Fly!*

2009. Illus., David Walker. Somerville, MA: Candlewick Press.

Summary: Baby animals learn how to fly, swim, and wiggle with a little help from their mothers.

Action: Guide the children in acting out the motions of the baby animals along with them:

- Bird—Flap your arms as if you are flying.
- Fish—Put your hands together in front of you and wiggle them like a fish swimming.
- Snake—Stand straight with your arms by your sides and wiggle.
- Otter—Hold your arms out in front of you and run in place like you are getting ready to slide.
- Duck—Hold your hands out in front of you and flap them back and forth like duck feet swimming through water.
- Mouse—Squish down close to the floor to be small like a mouse.
- Child—Act however you want.
- For a little more movement, hold your hand above your eyes like you are looking at something far away whenever a baby animal says "I see a . . ."

———. *Toot Toot Zoom!*

2009. Illus., Matthew Cordell. Somerville, MA: Candlewick Press.

Summary: Pierre drives over the mountain looking for friends and unknowingly finds some along the way.

Action: Act out the motions and sounds of Pierre's car as he drives up and over the mountain. Whenever you read the following words, have the children do the corresponding actions:

- "Toot"—Pretend to honk a horn.
- "Zoom"—Pretend to hold a steering wheel with your hands and run quickly in place.

- "Screech"—Lean back as if you are quickly stomping on brakes.
- "Huff" and "Puff"—Pretend to push the heavy car to the top of the hill.
- "Smash," "Crash," and "Bash"—Fall to the ground as the car crashes.

———. *Creak! Said the Bed.*

2010. Illus., Regan Dunnick. Somerville, MA: Candlewick Press.

Summary: On a dark and stormy night, all of the family members climb into one bed, but it finally breaks under the weight.

Action: Have everyone stand up at the beginning of this book. Whenever someone new enters the bedroom, the door goes "Squeak." Everyone should pretend to push open a door and say "Squeak." When the bed finally cracks, fall to the floor.

Rueda, Claudia. *Let's Play in the Forest While the Wolf Is Not Around.*

2006. New York: Scholastic Press.

Summary: The other animals play while Wolf gets ready for school.

Action: Get ready along with Wolf. Have the children pretend to put on their underpants, undershirts, pants, T-shirts, socks, shoes, and jackets, and then comb their hair and put on their backpacks. Finally, when Wolf is hungry and wants to eat, the children can rub their tummies.

Sartell, Debra. *Time for Bed, Baby Ted.*

2010. Illus., Kay Chorao. New York: Holiday House.

Summary: Baby Ted pretends to be many different animals as his father gets him ready for bed.

Action: Tell the children to pretend to be the different animals along with Baby Ted:

- Crocodile—Hold your arms out straight, one up high and the other low; then clap them together quickly like a crocodile closing its mouth.
- Duck—Flap your arms like wings and quack.
- Frog—Jump up and down.
- Bat—Bend at your waist so that you are upside down and flap your arms like wings.

- Penguin—Bounce from one foot to the other like a penguin waddle.
- Mouse—Crouch down to the floor to make yourself seem very small.
- Chicken—Make a beak by holding out two fingers and your thumb and cluck as you hold your beak near your mouth.
- Owl—Flap your arms like wings and turn your head as far as it will go from side to side.
- Seal—Hold your arms out straight in front of you and clap them together like a seal.
- Porcupine—Use one finger to poke into the air like a porcupine quill.

Schaefer, Carole Lexa. *Dragon Dancing.*

2007. Illus., Pierr Morgan. New York: Viking.

   Summary: A class decorates a dragon for Mei Lin's birthday and then each of them pretends to be part of the dragon.

   Action: When the children are done creating their dragon, they line up to go "Dragon Dancing." At that point, get everyone into one line and weave around the room as you finish the story. If you have time to have everyone create a dragon mask, you can continue to parade after the story throughout the rest of the library.

Schwarz, Viviane. *There Are No Cats in This Book.*

2010. Somerville, MA: Candlewick Press.

   Summary: Three cats decide to leave their book to see the world.

   Action: Help the cats leave the book by having the children act out the motions with them:

- Push—Put your hands out in front of you and pretend to push on something very hard.
- Jump—Jump up high to get out of the book.
- Wish—Close your eyes tight and make a wish.
- Finally, when the cats bring friends back with them, wave to all of the new cats in the book.

Sklansky, Amy E. *The Duck Who Played the Kazoo.*

2008. Illus., Tiphanie Beeke. New York: Clarion Books.

   Summary: A kazoo-playing duck leaves his lake to find friends.

Action: The duck plays his kazoo "zu zu" on almost every double-page spread of this book. Whenever he plays his kazoo, have the children put one hand near their mouths like they are playing kazoos and say "zu zu" along with him.

Stanley, Mandy. *Lettice the Flying Rabbit.*

2003. New York: Simon and Schuster Books for Young Readers.

Summary: Lettice wants to fly and gets her wish when she climbs into a remote-controlled airplane.

Action: Tell the children to try to fly with Lettice: flap your arms, flap your ears, and flap your "whiskers and tail." Finally, when Lettice flies in the remote-controlled airplane, have the children hold their arms out to the sides and fly around the room. Then have everyone settle down for the rest of the story.

Stein, David Ezra. *Pouch!*

2009. New York: G. P. Putnam's Sons.

Summary: A brand-new kangaroo is afraid of the other animals he meets outside of his mother's pouch until he meets another baby kangaroo.

Action: Join Joey on his quest for independence. The first time he jumps out of his mother's pouch, he hops twice before meeting a bee and returning to the safety of the pouch. Have the children jump forward twice with Joey and then backward once to return to the pouch. The second time, Joey hops three times before getting scared. The children should jump the same number of times Joey hops in each scene. Finally, when he finds a friend, everyone can hop all around the room.

Stiegemeyer, Julie. *Cheep! Cheep!*

2006. Illus., Carol Baicker-McKee. New York: Bloomsbury Publishing.

Summary: Three chicks celebrate the arrival of a new chick.

Action: Help the children to act out the motions with the chicks in this book:

- "Sleep"—Lay your head on your hands like you are sleeping.
- "Cheep"—Flap your arms like a chicken and say "Cheep."
- "Peep?"—Open one eye as if you were sleeping and heard a noise.
- "Cheep?"—Hold your arms out like you are asking a question.
- "Creep"—Slowly creep to one side.
- "Eep!"—Look over the edge.

- "Leap!"—Jump up in the air.
- "Heap!"—Fall on the ground.
- "Cheep"—Flap your arms like a chicken again.
- "Sleep"—Lay your head on your hands like you are sleeping again.

Sturges, Philemon. *How Do You Make a Baby Smile?*

2007. Illus., Bridget Strevens-Marzo. New York: HarperCollins.

Summary: Make a baby smile, laugh, coo, and grin by doing funny things like animals do.

Action: Have the children do the motions along with the animals in this book:

- Crocodile—Smile big.
- Elephant—Wiggle your ears.
- Deer—Open your hands wide, place them on top of your head like antlers, and shake your head.
- Giraffe—Turn your head side to side.
- Baboon—Make a funny face.
- Raccoon—Place your hands in front of your face and play peekaboo.
- Robin—Sing a song together.
- Chicken—Cluck like a chicken and wave your arms like wings.
- Cricket—Rub your legs together to pretend to make cricket music.
- Big sister—Tickle your chin.

Suen, Anastasia. *Subway.*

2004. Illus., Karen Katz. New York: Viking.

Summary: A young girl and her mother enjoy a ride on a subway.

Action: Each page of this text has action words that you and the children can do along with the girl and her mother:

- "down, down, down"—Start standing up straight and slowly lower yourself down toward the ground.
- "walk, walk, walk"—Walk in place.
- "hop, hop, hop"—Hop on one foot or jump.
- "go, go, go"—Run quickly in place.
- "ride, ride, ride"—Sit down and sway with the train cars.
- "step, step, step"—Pretend to walk upstairs.

- "play, play, play"—Hold a pretend saxophone and say "La La La."
- "night, night, night"—Since we sleep at night, lay your head on your hands as if you are going to sleep.
- "wind, wind, wind"—Wave your arms in the air like trees blowing in the wind.
- "more, more, more"—Squish everyone together as if they are on a crowded subway car.
- "rock, rock, rock"—Hold your arm up in the air as if you are holding a subway bar and sway with the car's motion.
- "flash, flash, flash"—Close your hands into fists and open them three times like lights flashing.
- "blur, blur, blur"—Wave your open hands in front of your face to make everything blurry.
- "bye, bye, bye"—Wave good-bye.

Suen, Anastasia. *Red Light, Green Light.*

2005. Illus., Ken Wilson-Max. Orlando: Harcourt.

Summary: A young boy takes his toy cars on an imaginary trip.

Action: Have the children pretend to drive cars along with the child. Tell them to hold their hands out like they are holding steering wheels. When the car is moving, the children can walk or run in place. They should stop walking or running for the red light, the railroad tracks, and to pay the toll.

Tankard, Jeremy. *Grumpy Bird.*

2007. New York: Scholastic Press.

Summary: Bird wakes up grumpy but cheers up after a silly walk with friends.

Action: Take the children on a walk along with Bird. Pause to read each page, but then walk around the room for a few seconds with Bird. Have the children play along with Bird when he stops walking—stand on one leg, jump, and flap their arms to fly back to Bird's nest.

Teckentrup, Britta. *Little Wolf's Song.*

2010. London: Boxer Books.

Summary: Little Wolf has trouble learning how to howl until he needs to when he is lost.

Action: Little Wolf howls three times in this book. Each time he howls, have the children tilt their heads back and howl along with him.

Thompson, Lauren. *Little Quack's New Friend.*

2006. Illus., Derek Anderson. New York: Simon and Schuster Books for Young Readers.

> **Summary:** Little Quack plays with a frog and his siblings finally join in when they see how much fun they are having.

> **Action:** Have the children play along with Little Quack and Little Ribbit:

- "Splishy, splosh!"—Flap your arms and hands around like you are splashing in water.
- "Squashy, squooshy, squash!"—Play in the mud by jumping and then slowly lifting your legs like you are stuck in mud.
- "Boingo, poingo, boingo, poing!"—Bounce and jump around.
- "Plunka, splunka, plunka, splunka, plunk!"—Bend at your waist like you are diving under water like a duck.

———. *Wee Little Bunny.*

2010. Illus., John Butler. New York: Simon and Schuster Books for Young Readers.

> **Summary:** A brand-new bunny tries to experience everything in a single day.

> **Action:** Encourage the children to play along with the bunny:

- "run, run, run!"—Run in place.
- "giggle, giggle, giggle!"—Hold your sides as you laugh loudly.
- "tippy-tippy-toe!"—Walk on your tiptoes.
- "wiggle, wiggle, wiggle!"—Wiggle your whole body.
- "fast, fast, fast!"—Run really fast in place.
- "snuggle, snuggle, snuggle!"—Settle back down into a comfortable sitting position.

Trapani, Iza. *Froggie Went A-Courtin'.*

2002. Watertown, MA: Whispering Coyote.

> **Summary:** Froggie proposes to many ladies before finding the right one for him.

> **Action:** Whenever Froggie proposes to another animal, have the kids get down on one knee as if they are proposing to someone. When the animal says no, the children should stand up and shake their heads.

Tullet, Hervé. *Press Here.*

2010. San Francisco: Handprint Books.

Summary: An imaginative play on interactive books.

Action: Have the children join you in playing along with the book:

- When the book tells you to press or tap a particular color, hold your palm out and pretend to push a button in front of you.
- When the book tells you to rub a dot, hold your palm out and turn it in a slow circle.
- When the book tells you to shake the book, shake your whole body.
- When the book tells you to tilt the book to one side or the other, tilt your whole body.
- When the book tells you to blow on the dots, blow up into the air.
- When the book tells you to stand it up straight, stand as straight and tall as you can.
- When the book tells you to clap your hands, clap the number of times specified.

van Rossum, Heleen. *Will You Carry Me?*

2005. Illus., Peter van Harmelen. La Jolla, CA: Kane/Miller.

Summary: When Thomas becomes too tired to walk home, his mother finds other fun ways to finish the journey.

Action: Take the children on a journey along with Thomas and his mother:

- Jump—Jump around the room.
- Swim—Pretend you are swimming around the room.
- Fly—Hold your arms out and fly around the room.
- Run—Run around the room.

Do each of these motions for a few seconds after his mother suggests the action. Then pause to continue reading.

Waddell, Martin. *Hi, Harry!*

2003. Illus., Barbara Firth. Cambridge, MA: Candlewick Press.

Summary: Harry the turtle finally finds a friend who moves as slowly as he does.

Action: Buster Rabbit, Stan Badger, and Sarah Mouse all rush by Harry as he tries to find a friend. Have the children join you in imitating the movements in the story. As each animal runs past, run quickly in place. When Harry sets off to find a friend, walk very slowly in place. Finally, play with Harry and Sam Snail by walking very slowly and then holding your hands in the air in triumph as you win the race, sticking your head out far and then pulling it back, and turning in a very slow circle.

Walton, Rick. *Bunnies on the Go.*

2003. Illus., Paige Miglio. New York: HarperCollins.

Summary: A family of bunnies uses a variety of different forms of transportation on their vacation.

Action: Have the children pretend to ride in all of the forms of transportation along with the bunnies:

- Car—Hold a pretend steering wheel.
- Train—Hold your arms at your sides, bend them at the elbow, and then move them in circles like the wheels of a train.
- Wagon—Hold pretend reins and bounce your hands up and down as you coax the horse to move forward.
- Tractor—Bounce up and down.
- Balloon—Hold your arms in a circle above your head as if your arms are the balloon and your body is the basket.
- Boat—Put on a pretend life jacket.
- Bikes—Put on a pretend helmet.
- Truck—Hold a pretend steering wheel and bounce up and down on the bumpy road.
- Bus—Sit down and pretend to sleep on the bus.
- Ferry—Sway with the waves on the ferry.
- Cab—Climb in the back of the cab and pay the driver.
- Plane—Hold your arms out and fly through the air.

Ward, Jennifer. *Way Up in the Arctic.*

2007. Illus., Kenneth J. Spengler. Flagstaff, AZ: Rising Moon.

Summary: Arctic animal mothers and their babies play and cuddle together.

Action: Encourage the children to play along with the animals in this book:

- Prance with the caribou—Hold your hands up on your head like antlers and gallop.
- Nap with the polar bear—Curl up on the floor to take a nap.
- Sing with the beluga—Sing "la la la."
- Wobble with the walrus—Hold your hands down by your sides like flippers and wobble side to side.
- Jump with the hare—Jump in place.
- Dive with the seal—Hold your arms above your head as if you are taking a dive.
- Prowl with the wolf—Creep around like you are stealthily hunting something.
- Hoot with the owl—Say "whooo" like an owl.
- Dig with the lemming—Bend down and pretend to dig into the floor.
- Cuddle with the fox—Go and hug the adult who brought you to storytime.

Warhola, James. *If You're Happy and You Know It.*

2007. New York: Orchard Books.

Summary: Jungle animals sing this children's song about ways that they show happiness.

Action: Show the children how to do the motions with the animals:

- Clap your hands with the child.
- Stomp your feet with the elephant—Stomp your great big feet.
- Scratch your fur with the monkey—Scratch under your arms like a monkey.
- Give a roar with the lion—Roar loudly.
- Flap your wings with the bird—Hold your arms out straight and flap them like they are wings.
- Laugh out loud with the hyena—Hold your sides as you laugh loudly.
- Beat your chest with the gorilla—Make your hands into fists and softly hit your chest with one hand at a time.
- Jump up high with the frog—Jump as high as you can.
- Crawl around with the snake—Crawl on the floor or pretend to slither like a snake.
- Blink your eyes with the toucan—Blink both eyes.

Watson, Richard Jesse. *The Magic Rabbit.*

2005. New York: The Blue Sky Press.

Summary: A rabbit pops out of a magic hat and tries to find a friend.

Action: Together with the children, act like the animals that pop out of the hat:

- Rabbit—Hop out of the hat by jumping up high.
- Frog—Jump away by jumping three times in place.
- Mice—Scurry away by running in place.
- Birds—Fly away by flapping your arms like wings.
- Another rabbit—Again, hop out of the hat by jumping up high.

Wattenberg, Jane. *Henny-Penny.*

2000. New York: Scholastic Press.

Summary: A retelling of the classic story of the chicken telling everyone that the sky is falling.

Action: Henny-Penny and her friends run to tell the king that the sky is falling. Whenever a new character joins them, have the children run quickly in place. When they all meet up with Foxy-Loxy, he plays a trick on them and gobbles them up in his den. When Foxy-Loxy eats the other birds, the children should open their arms wide like a great big mouth and gobble them up with Foxy-Loxy. Finally, they can run quickly in place while Henny-Penny runs home.

Weeks, Sarah. *Oh My Gosh, Mrs. McNosh!*

2002. Illus., Nadine Bernard Westcott. New York: Laura Geringer Books.

Summary: Mrs. McNosh's dog breaks his leash and she chases him all over town.

Action: Have the children help Mrs. McNosh chase after her dog. Once the leash breaks and her dog runs away, have the children run in place to try to catch him. When she finally gives up and goes home, the children should walk very slowly in place.

Whippo, Walt. *Little White Duck.*

2000. Illus., Joan Paley. Boston: Little, Brown.

Summary: A duck, frog, bug, snake, and narrator mouse have fun in a pond.

Action: Have the children play in the pond along with the animals:

- Duck—Pretend to take a bite of the lily pad.
- Frog—Jump off the lily pad.

- Bug—Pretend to tickle the frog by tickling yourself.
- Snake—Scare the other animals by making a scary face.
- Mouse—Pretend to wipe your eyes from crying because everyone else has left the pond.

Willis, Jeanne. *That's Not Funny!*

2010. Illus., Adrian Reynolds. London: Andersen Press.

Summary: Hyena plays a trick on giraffe and then laughs at the results, but finally gets a taste of his own medicine.

Action: Whenever Hyena laughs, have the children hold their sides and laugh loudly with him. When Hyena ends up on the other end of the trick, everyone should laugh even louder.

Wojtusik, Elizabeth. *Kitty Up!*

2008. Illus., Sachiko Yoshikawa. New York: Dial Books for Young Readers.

Summary: A kitten has an adventurous day both inside and outside of the house.

Action: You and the children can play along with the kitten on most of the pages in this book:

- "Kitty up"—Act like you are jumping up onto something.
- "Kitty down"—Act like you are jumping off of something.
- "Kitty fast"—Run quickly in place.
- "Kitty slow"—Walk very slowly in place.
- "Kitty stop"—Freeze.
- "Kitty go"—Run quickly in place again.
- "Kitty leap"—Jump.
- "Kitty still"—Freeze.
- "Kitty will"—Pretend to jump off the windowsill.
- "Kitty hunt"—Pretend to chase after another animal.
- "Kitty creep"—Walk on your tiptoes.
- "Kitty sleep"—Curl up on the floor.
- "Kitty wake"—Stand back up.
- "Kitty scream"—Meow loudly.
- "Kitty lost"—Look around like you don't recognize anything.
- "Kitty peek"—Hold your hand up above your eyes as you search far away.
- "Kitty gasp"—Gasp out loud.

- "Kitty shriek"—Meow again.
- "Kitty listen"—Hold your hand up to one ear.
- "Kitty hear"—Hold your hand up to your other ear.
- "Kitty cheer"—Meow happily.
- "Kitty end"—Sit back down on the floor.

Yolen, Jane. *Off We Go!*

2000. Illus., Laurel Molk. Boston: Little, Brown.

Summary: Woodland creatures all go visit Grandma in their own special way.

Action: Take the children on a trip to visit Grandma with the animals:

- "Tip-toe" with the mouse—Walk very quietly on your tiptoes.
- "Hip-hop" with the frog—Jump like a frog by bending your knees, putting your hands on the floor between your legs, and jumping into the air.
- "Dig-deep" with the mole—Crouch down and pretend to dig into the floor.
- "Slither-slee" with the snake—Hold your arms down straight by your sides and slither your body back and forth.
- "Scritch-scratch" with the duck—Hold your arms out like wings while you waddle like a duck.
- "Creep-crawl" with the spider—Bend over and walk on your hands and your feet.
- Then do all of the motions one after another as you continue on your way to Grandma's house.

Yolen, Jane. *Hoptoad.*

2003. Illus., Karen Lee Schmidt. San Diego: Harcourt.

Summary: A toad tries to cross the road, almost gets run over by a truck, and makes it to safety with some help.

Action: Have the children cross the road with the toad. They can jump up high whenever the toad hops.

Ziefert, Harriet. *Zoo Parade!*

2003. Illus., Simms Taback. Maplewood, NJ: Blue Apple Books.

Summary: Each animal walks to the zoo in its own special way.

Action: Show the children how to walk to the zoo like the different animals:

- Leap like a tiger—Leap forward once.
- Tiptoe like an elephant—Walk carefully with your big feet.
- Race like a leopard—Run quickly in place.
- Prance like a lion—Stand up tall, hold your hands out wide around your face like a mane, and walk slowly.
- Dance like a gazelle—Dance anyway you like.
- Run like a baboon—Run quickly in place.
- Gallop like a zebra—Gallop around the room.
- Swing like a monkey—Hold one hand up in the air as if you are holding a branch and move back and forth.
- Saunter like a giraffe—Hold your neck very tall while you walk.
- Jump like a kangaroo—Jump in place.
- March like a camel—March in place.

Zimmerman, Andrea, and David Clemesha. *Dig!*

2004. Illus., Marc Rosenthal. Orlando: Harcourt.

Summary: Mr. Rally and his dog take their backhoe to five digging jobs.

Action: Dig along with Mr. Rally. Whenever he digs at one of his five jobs, have the children pretend to dig into the floor with their hands. At the end of each job, this question is asked: "Is all the digging done?" Have the children shake their heads and say "No" loudly along with the book.

props

Scarves and puppets!

A juggling scarf can be a cape or a blanket or a washcloth or a pillow. The kids in your program can become active participants when they interact with a tactile part of the story you are reading. You'll feel the excitement in the room as the kids anxiously wait to use their prop. The stories included in this chapter have multiple pieces so everyone can help tell the story. Instructions on how to make homemade props are also included where applicable.

tips

- Ask the adults in the room to participate with the children. If you have enough props, give one to each adult to encourage participation.
- When using props such as juggling scarves or rhythm sticks, model the movements as much as possible when you are reading books such as *Like a Windy Day* or *Not a Stick*.
- Put the props in only part of the room for books such as *The Magic Toolbox*. Do this if you want the kids to use the props only during certain parts of the story. When you are done using the blocks in this story, everyone can move back to the regular storytime space.

- Have extra stuffed animals/dolls available for kids who forget to bring their own for books such as *Mama's Day*. Be sure to remind your group the week before to bring their favorite stuffed animals or dolls.
- Ask the kids to put their props on the floor in front of them until you are ready to use them. This can be useful for books such as *The Little Yellow Leaf* when the kids are tempted to play with the scarves early in the book.
- It is okay for the kids to interact with the props the whole time for books such as *One Monday*. In other books, if you are comfortable having them interact with the props throughout the whole story, let them.
- Use masking tape to create a circle on the floor for books such as *I Took the Moon for a Walk*. Ask the children to stand on the tape to create a group circle. You can also use a rug and ask the children to stand on the edge of the rug to create a circle.
- Practice movements before you read the book. In books such as *Thanks, Mom*, practice running in place for a few seconds. Or for books such as *Big Chickens Fly the Coop*, practice waving the paper chickens in the air.
- During some of the stories, such as *Super Sam!*, it may be easier to let the kids stand during the entire story. Be sure to stand up as well so that everyone can see the story.
- Include clean-up time at the end of any story with a prop. Have everyone return their props to you before you continue with the next story.

Anderson, Derek. *Blue Burt and Wiggles.*

2006. New York: Simon and Schuster Books for Young Readers.

Summary: Blue Burt the bird and Wiggles the worm try to stop winter from coming.

Action: Cut out flannel shapes of a tree, leaves, grass, flowers, the sun, and clouds. Make sure you have enough for every child to have one shape. Put the tree shape on your flannel board. When Blue Burt and Wiggles tape the leaves to the branches, have the kids add the leaf shapes to the flannel board. When they paint the grass, add the grass shapes to your flannel board. When they paint flowers on construction paper, add the flower shapes to the flannel board. Finally, when they hang a sun and white clouds from the trees, add those shapes to the flannel board. When Blue Burt and Wiggles climb down to admire all of their work, knock everything off of the flannel board.

Anderson, Peggy Perry. *Chuck's Truck.*

2006. Boston: Houghton Mifflin.

Summary: Chuck and the farm animals ride to town in his old truck, but it breaks down along the way.

Action: Hand out stuffed animals for all of the farm animal characters in this story. Have a truck, a wagon, or a box available. As each animal gets in the truck in the story, have the child with that stuffed animal add it to the toy truck.

Araki, Mie. *The Magic Toolbox.*

2003. San Francisco: Chronicle Books.

Summary: Lulu builds with blocks, but Fred's creations fall down until he finds a magic toolbox.

Action: Put out blocks and let the kids build their own creations as you read. Or have them build the creations on each page and pause to let them work before moving on. Have even more fun by knocking down the buildings just like Fred's house. Of course, you'll want to be careful during the knocking-down phase so that no one gets hurt.

Asch, Frank, and Devin Asch. *Like a Windy Day.*

2002. San Diego: Gulliver Books.

Summary: A young girl's imagination helps her play like the wind.

Action: Give the children juggling scarves that they can wave in the wind as you read this book. On some pages you can be more specific with the motions:

- "and snap wet sheets"—Snap the scarf quickly.
- "I want to lift birds and butterflies in the sky"—Throw the scarf up in the air.
- "I want to steal hats"—Wear the scarf like a hat.

Ashman, Linda. *Mama's Day.*

2006. Illus., Jan Ormerod. New York: Simon and Schuster Books for Young Readers.

Summary: Mama and her child have many adventures throughout the day.

Action: This book works best if you have the children bring their favorite stuffed animals to storytime. Their animals will act as their "babies." As you read, they can act out the story with their babies—lift the baby from a crib, teach the baby how to clap, share snacks with the baby, give the baby a bath, and so forth.

Asquith, Ros. *Baby's Shoe.*

2005. Illus., Sam Childs. London: Hutchinson.

Summary: Many farm animals help a child look for baby's shoe.

Action: Get a stuffed cock, duck, cow, horse, dog, sheep, and pig, or make pictures of the seven animals. Hand out the props before reading the story. Walk around the room as you read this book so you can search for baby's shoe. As each animal joins the story, have the child with that animal follow you around the room.

Baddiel, Ivor, and Sophie Jubb. *Cock-a-Doodle Quack! Quack!*

2007. Illus., Ailie Busby. Oxford: David Fickling Books.

Summary: A baby rooster gets help from the other farm animals as he learns to cock-a-doodle-doo.

Action: Create a picture of each of the helper animals in this book (pig, cow, duck, cat, and owl). Tape the animals to the walls of your programming space. As the rooster talks to each animal, have the kids walk over to that animal with you. The kids can also help answer the "What do you say?" question. You can add extra interaction by asking the kids if they think the animals wake up when the rooster says the wrong thing.

Baker, Keith. *Just How Long Can a Long String Be?!*

2009. New York: Arthur A. Levine Books.

Summary: A bird shows an ant how many different ways a long piece of string can be used.

Action: Give each child a one- or two-foot piece of yarn. As you read the story, have the children act out the different ways to use the string. For example, they can hold the string up as if there is a balloon on the other end, let it fly in the sky as it holds onto a kite, use it like a mop, and go fishing with it.

Beaumont, Karen. *Duck, Duck, Goose! (A Coyote's on the Loose!)*

2004. Illus., Jose Aruego and Ariane Dewey. New York: HarperCollins.

Summary: Many different animals try to outrun a monster.

Action: Create a flannel-board piece for all of the animals in this book (duck, goose, pig, pup, cow, goat, sheep, mouse, chick, hen, cat, and rabbit). Hand out all of the animals, except for the rabbit, to the children in your program. As each animal enters the story, have that child come to the front of the room and add his or her animal to the flannel board. When the rabbit enter the story, add it to the flannel board to show that there isn't really a "monster."

———. *Move Over, Rover!*

2006. Illus., Jane Dyer. Orlando: Harcourt.

> **Summary:** Many different animals join Rover in his doghouse to escape the storm.
>
> **Action:** Have a stuffed animal for all of the animals in the book (dog, cat, raccoon, squirrel, blue jay, snake, mouse, and skunk) and a box barely big enough to fit them all. Give out the stuffed animals to kids in your program before you start to read. As each animal enters the story, have the child with that animal put the stuffed animal in the box (doghouse). When all of the animals scatter, dump out the box and have the child with the skunk put that stuffed animal in the box.

Berger, Carin. *The Little Yellow Leaf.*

2008. New York: Greenwillow Books.

> **Summary:** A little yellow leaf holds on to a tree branch and finally lets go with another leaf.
>
> **Action:** Give the children juggling scarves that they can hold as their leaves. When the two leaves finally let go, have the children throw their "leaves" in the air.

Curtis, Carolyn. *I Took the Moon for a Walk.*

2004. Illus., Alison Jay. Cambridge, MA: Barefoot Books.

> **Summary:** A young boy goes on an adventurous walk with the moon watching over him.
>
> **Action:** Give each child a round piece of paper (the moon), which has been glued onto a Popsicle stick. Have the children form a circle. Read the first page and then have the children hold up their moons and walk a few steps around the circle. Continue walking the paper moons after every page.

Dobbins, Jan. *Driving My Tractor.*

2009. Illus., David Sim. Cambridge, MA: Barefoot Books.

Summary: A farmer and his animals travel down a bumpy road.

Action: Create a truck out of felt for your flannel board. Put the truck on the board before you start to read. Also create felt pieces for all of the animals in the book: one black-and-white cow, two grey donkeys, three pink pigs, four white lambs, and five brown chickens. Pass out the animals to the children in your program. As each animal comes into the story, have the child with that animal add his or her piece to the flannel board.

Emberley, Ed. *Thanks, Mom.*

2003. Boston: Little, Brown.

Summary: A hungry mouse is chased by a cat, who is chased by a dog, who is chased by a larger animal, and so forth.

Action: Give each child something small to represent the cheese (a piece of yellow foam, paper, or felt will work). The words "Run, Kiko, run!" appear six times in the text. Each time you read those words, have the kids run really fast in place without dropping their pieces of "cheese."

Gorbachev, Valeri. *One Rainy Day.*

2002. New York: Philomel Books.

Summary: A pig is joined under a tree by many other animals in order to escape the rain.

Action: Print or create a picture of all of the animals in this book: one pig, one mouse, two porcupines, three buffaloes, four leopards, five lions, six gorillas, seven crocodiles, eight hippopotamuses, nine rhinoceroses, and ten elephants. You can choose whether to make one picture (i.e., two porcupines on one piece of paper) or multiple pictures (i.e., two separate porcupine pictures) based on the size of your group. Give each child one of the pictures. Open an umbrella and put it on the floor in the front of the room. As each animal runs under the tree, have the child (or children) with that picture add his or her animal under the umbrella.

Graham, Bob. *Max.*

2000. Cambridge, MA: Candlewick Press.

Summary: Max has trouble learning to fly like the rest of his superhero family.

Action: Give every child a juggling scarf. Have them hold the scarves over their shoulders like capes. Each time Max tries to fly, the children can jump up in the air to learn to fly with him. When he finally does fly, the children can keep holding the scarves and "fly" around the room.

Helakoski, Leslie. *Big Chickens Fly the Coop.*

2008. Illus., Henry Cole. New York: Dutton Children's Books.

> **Summary:** Four chickens have many adventures on their way to the farmhouse.
>
> **Action:** Give each child a die-cut chicken shape attached to a Popsicle stick. When the four chickens go wild reacting to the doghouse, tractor, and barn, have the kids hold their chickens in the air and wave them around frantically until the chickens in the story return to their coop.

Hest, Amy. *Little Chick.*

2009. Illus., Anita Jeram. Somerville, MA: Candlewick Press.

> **Summary:** Three stories about Little Chick and her Old-Auntie. In the middle story, she finally gets a kite to fly.
>
> **Action:** Give the children juggling scarves that they can use as their kites. As Little Chick tries to fly her kite, the kids can hold their scarves up in the air. When Little Chick's kite finally takes flight, the kids can throw their scarves in the air to simulate many flying kites.

Hillenbrand, Will. *My Book Box.*

2006. Orlando: Harcourt.

> **Summary:** An elephant explores the many different ways to use a box and decides the best use is to fill it with books.
>
> **Action:** Before you start reading the story, have every child pick a book off the shelves. If your storytime space is in another part of the library, bring a cart of books for them to pick from. Bring a large box (or two if needed) and place it on the floor in front of you. When you get to the part of the story where the elephant chooses to use the box as a book box, ask the children to come up to the front to put their books in your box. Then continue the story.

Himmelman, John. *Chickens to the Rescue.*

2006. New York: Henry Holt.

> **Summary:** Chickens save the day Monday through Saturday on the farm.
>
> **Action:** Give each child a die-cut chicken shape glued to a Popsicle stick. Every time you read "Chickens to the rescue!" have the kids wave their

chickens around and cluck. On Sunday, when the chickens rest, have the kids lay their chickens down to sleep.

———. *Katie Loves the Kittens.*

2008. New York: Henry Holt.

Summary: Katie has difficulty hiding her excitement when three kittens join the family.

Action: Give each child a die-cut dog shape glued to a Popsicle stick. When Katie gets excited and barks around the kittens, have the kids wave their dogs around and howl with Katie. When Katie finally figures out how to control her excitement, have the kids pet their dogs.

Horáček, Petr. *When the Moon Smiled.*

2003. Cambridge, MA: Candlewick Press.

Summary: The moon slowly lights the stars to wake up the night animals and help the day animals go to sleep.

Action: Give each child a star cut out of felt. When the moon lights a star for the dog, have one child put a star on your felt flannel board. When the moon lights a star for the cats, have another child put a star on the flannel board. Continue adding stars until you get to the tenth star for the moths. On the final page, have all of the children who still have stars bring theirs up for a full night sky.

Howie. Betsy. *The Block Mess Monster.*

2008. Illus., C. B. Decker. New York: Henry Holt.

Summary: The Block Mess Monster does not want Calpurnia to clean her room until her mother asks it to help.

Action: Set out a bunch of blocks for the kids to use while you read the story. Ask them to build their own Block Mess Monsters. On the page where the mother asks the monster to climb up onto a shelf, have the kids clean up the blocks as if their monsters are also ready to be put away. If you don't have enough blocks for kids to build something, you can give just one block to each child to put away.

Huntington, Amy. *One Monday.*

2001. New York: Orchard Books.

Summary: The wind on this farm gets stronger every day until it blows itself out on Sunday.

Action: Give each child a juggling scarf. As you read the story, have the kids swirl their scarves around with the wind. On Sunday, when "the wind blew so hard, it simply blew itself right out of town," have the kids throw their scarves up in the air.

Hutchins, Pat. *We're Going on a Picnic!*

2002. New York: Greenwillow Books.

Summary: A hen, duck, and goose go on a picnic, but their food is stolen along the way.

Action: Split the group into three sections. Give each child in one section a plastic berry. In another section, give them all a plastic apple. In the last section, give them all a plastic pear. If you do not have plastic fruit, you can give them all a piece of felt or paper cut into the correct shape. Put a basket large enough to hold everything next to you. When Hen picks berries, have all of the kids with berries add their fruit to the basket. Do the same when Goose picks apples and Duck picks pears. The first time the trio puts down their basket, bring out a stuffed squirrel. Have one group come up and take one piece of fruit each out of the basket and go sit back down. Bring out a chipmunk and a rabbit the next two times that the trio puts down their basket. Again have one group come up to take fruit out of the basket for the chipmunk and the other group come up for the rabbit. When the chicken, duck, and goose realize that their basket is empty and decide to pick more fruit, have the kids come up and put their fruit back in the basket.

Isadora, Rachel. *Peekaboo Bedtime.*

2008. New York: G. P. Putnam's Sons.

Summary: A toddler plays peekaboo with family members and objects at bedtime.

Action: Give the children juggling scarves. As you read the story, have them play peekaboo every time you read "Peekaboo! I see . . ."

Jarman, Julia. *Big Red Tub.*

2004. Illus., Adrian Reynolds. New York: Orchard Books.

Summary: Two children have fun splashing in the tub with their animal friends.

Action: Give some of the children stuffed animals or pictures of the following animals: dog, lion, duck, turtle, penguin, giraffe, hippopotamus, kangaroo, and flamingo. Put a box or other container near you and pretend it is the bathtub. As each animal joins the story, have the child with that animal put it in the box. Everyone can pretend to splash along with Stan and Stella as you read the story.

Johnson, Kelly. *Look at the Baby.*

2002. New York: Henry Holt.

Summary: A celebration of babies and their cute bodies.

Action: A week in advance, ask the children to bring their favorite stuffed animals to storytime. As you read the book, have them point to the body parts on their stuffed animals: nose, fingers (paws), toes, chin, tummy, legs, eyes, and feet. You may want to have a couple of extra stuffed animals on hand in case anyone forgets to bring one.

Johnson, Paul Brett. *Little Bunny Foo Foo.*

2004. New York: Scholastic Press.

Summary: A twist on the classic children's song.

Action: Give each child a die-cut bunny shape glued onto a Popsicle stick. When you read/sing "Little Bunny Foo Foo hoppin' through the forest," have the kids hop their bunnies around. When you read/sing "Scoopin' up the field mice (woodchucks, foxes) and boppin' 'em on the head," have the kids make fists with their other hands and make the bunnies "bop" their fists. When you read/sing "Little Bunny Foo Foo I don't wanna see you scoopin' up the field mice (woodchucks, foxes) and boppin' 'em on the head," the kids should use their free hands to scold the bunnies with their pointer fingers.

Jones, Sylvie. *Who's in the Tub?*

2007. Illus., Pascale Constantin. Maplewood, NJ: Blue Apple Books.

Summary: A young boy doesn't want to take a bath with all of the animals in his tub, but ends up having a great time.

Action: Once Willy finally gets into the tub, give every child a juggling scarf. They can pretend the scarves are washcloths and scrub and play along with Willy.

Joyce, William. *Sleepy Time Olie.*

2001. New York: Laura Geringer Books.

> **Summary:** Rolie Polie Olie helps make Pappy feel better so everyone can sleep.
>
> **Action:** Have the kids sit in a circle. Put a few beach balls in the circle. Let the kids roll the balls to each other as you read this story.

> **alternate activity**
> Another option is to ask them to roll the balls only when you say the word *Rolie*.

Kimmelman, Leslie. *How Do I Love You?*

2006. Illus., Lisa McCue. New York: HarperCollins.

> **Summary:** A mother gives her child twenty different reasons why she loves him.
>
> **Action:** Hand out twenty felt alligator shapes to the children in your program. When you read that the mother loves her child "one in sunshine," have one child bring up an alligator shape to put on the flannel board. As a group, count to "one." When you read that the mother loves her child "two in snow," have another child add another alligator shape to the flannel board. As a group, count to "two." Continue all the way up to the twentieth reason.

Kopelke, Lisa. *Tissue, Please!*

2004. New York: Simon and Schuster Books for Young Readers.

> **Summary:** Frog and his friends discover that tissues are great for runny noses and can be artistic, too.
>
> **Action:** When you come to the part of the story where Frog's mother brings back a box of tissues, bring out your own box and give one tissue to each child. Have them hold onto the tissues until Frog is on stage and starts to wave his tissue above his head. Have them join frog in his tissue dance.

Lewis, Kim. *Here We Go, Harry.*

2005. Cambridge, MA: Candlewick Press.

> **Summary:** Harry and his friends jump and fly from the top of a hill on a windy day.
>
> **Action:** Give each child a juggling scarf. As you read the story, have the kids wave their scarves around like the wind is blowing them. When Lulu, Ted, and finally Harry jump and float in the air, have the kids throw their scarves in the air each time.

——. **Hooray for Harry.**

2006. Cambridge, MA: Candlewick Press.

Summary: Harry and his friends use his blanket in many imaginative games during the day, but then have to remember where they last left it.

Action: Give each child a juggling scarf. As you read the ways that Harry uses his blanket, have the children pretend to use the scarf in a similar way:

- When Harry uses his blanket as a tent, hold the scarf over your head like a tent.
- When Harry uses his blanket as a sail, hold the scarf out to the side and shake it slowly like a sail.
- When Harry uses his blanket as a swing, hold the scarf under you and pretend to swing back and forth.
- When Harry uses his blanket for a picnic, lay the scarf down and sit on it.
- When Harry washes his blanket, hold the scarf in between your hands as you pretend to wash it.
- When Harry remembers that his blanket is hanging to dry, hold the scarf tightly between two hands so it can dry.
- Finally, when Harry curls under his blanket, pretend that the scarf is a blanket.

——. **Seymour and Henry.**

2009. Somerville, MA: Candlewick Press.

Summary: Two ducks run off from their mother to play hide-and-seek, but run home when it starts to rain.

Action: Give every child two die-cut duck shapes. When Seymour and Henry hide, have the children hide their ducks behind their backs. When it starts to rain, have the children show their ducks, stand up, and run in place as Seymour and Henry run home.

Luebs, Robin. *Please Pick Me Up, Mama!*

2009. New York: Atheneum Books for Young Readers.

Summary: Little Raccoon asks her mama to pick her up and put her back down numerous times as she enjoys her day.

Action: Ask every child to bring a favorite stuffed animal to storytime. Each time Mama picks up Little Raccoon, have them pick up their animals.

Each time Mama puts her daughter back down, have them put their animals back on the floor.

McDonnell, Patrick. *Wag!*

2009. New York: Little, Brown.

Summary: Mooch knows why Earl's tail wags but it takes awhile to get the answer out.

Action: Give each child a juggling scarf. Ask them to hold the scarves at the base of their backs like tails. Whenever Earl wags his tail in the book, have the children shake and wag their "tails."

Meng, Cece. *Tough Chicks.*

2009. Illus., Melissa Suber. New York: Clarion Books.

Summary: Mama Hen's chicks don't act like the other chicks, but they save the day when the farmer's tractor stops working.

Action: Give every child a die-cut chick or chicken shape glued to a Popsicle stick. The three tough chicks "Peep, peep, zoom, zip, cheep" five times in the text. Every time you read those words, have the children make their chicks zoom around the space in front of them.

Meyers, Susan. *Everywhere Babies.*

2001. Illus., Marla Frazee. San Diego: Harcourt.

Summary: A description of what babies do and how people care for them.

Action: Ask everyone to bring a favorite stuffed animal or doll to storytime. Have a couple of extra stuffed animals available in case anyone forgets. The children can care for their babies like the babies in the book:

- Kiss the baby on its cheeks, ears, fingers, nose, head, tummy, and toes.
- Pretend to put clothes on the baby.
- Pretend to feed the baby.
- Rock the baby.
- Carry the baby around the room.
- Make the baby clap its hands.
- Play peekaboo with the baby.
- Hold the baby up to another baby (a friend's stuffed animal or doll) so they can make friends.
- Make the baby crawl.

- Make the baby walk.
- Give the baby a great big hug.

Middleton, Charlotte. *Nibbles: A Green Tale.*

2009. Tarrytown, NY: Marshall Cavendish Children.

Summary: Nibbles the guinea pig takes care of the last dandelion plant in town so that more dandelions can grow from its seeds.

Action: Nibbles cares for the dandelion plant until it turns into white seeds. At that point, give everyone pretend dandelion seeds. A handful of white confetti works perfectly. For a less messy approach, use juggling scarves or one white paper flower per child. When Nibbles goes to the top of the hill to blow the seeds into the air, have the kids blow their "seeds" around the room.

Murphy, Mary. *I Kissed the Baby!*

2003. Cambridge, MA: Candlewick Press.

Summary: Everyone is excited for the new baby duck and wants to be part of its life.

Action: Give everyone a die-cut duck shape. Have them act out the story with their ducks:

- "I saw the baby"—Hold up your baby duck for everyone to see.
- "I fed the baby"—Pretend to feed something to your duck.
- "I sang to the baby"—Sing "The Itsy Bitsy Spider" or "Row, Row, Row Your Boat" or another song to the baby ducks.
- "I tickled the baby"—Pretend to tickle the paper ducks.
- "I kissed the baby"—Kiss your baby duck.

Na, Il Sung. *The Thingamabob.*

2008. New York: Alfred A. Knopf.

Summary: An elephant finds an umbrella and tries to figure out what it is used for.

Action: Give every child a juggling scarf or a fancy drink umbrella. They can figure out how to use the scarves or umbrellas along with the elephant: pretend to fly with them; pretend to sit in them like boats; hold them in front of their faces to hide behind them; and finally, hold them over their heads to protect them from the rain.

Nakamura, Katherine Riley. *Song of Night: It's Time to Go to Bed.*

2002. Illus., Linnea Riley. New York: The Blue Sky Press.

Summary: A soothing story of nighttime rituals as baby animals get ready for bed.

Action: Ask everyone to bring in a favorite stuffed animal or doll. As you read the story, have the kids hold their animals or dolls in their arms and rock them to sleep.

Neitzel, Shirley. *I'm Not Feeling Well Today.*

2001. Illus., Nancy Winslow Parker. New York: Greenwillow Books.

Summary: A cumulative tale about a child who feels ill until he realizes it is a snow day.

Action: The child's first request in this tale is for "a box of tissues, in case I sneeze." At that point, give each of the children a real tissue and have them pretend to sneeze into it. There are ten references to the tissue box, so there will be lots of pretend sneezing.

Neubecker, Robert. *Beasty Bath.*

2005. New York: Orchard Books.

Summary: A little girl likes to pretend to be a beast while she takes a bath to get ready for bed.

Action: Give each child a juggling scarf. As the little girl takes a bath, they can pretend to wash their feet, claws (hands), fur and scales (body), horns (head), tails (bottom), and beasty mane (hair). Then they can use the scarves as towels to dry off.

Numeroff, Laura. *When Sheep Sleep.*

2006. Illus., David McPhail. New York: Abrams Books for Young Readers.

Summary: When a small child cannot count sheep because the sheep are already asleep, she tries counting other animals.

Action: Create a felt sheep, deer, cow, pig, puppy, bird, cat, bear, and rabbit. Hand the animals out to different children in the storytime. As the little girl tries to count each different animal, have the child with that animal come up and add it to your flannel board. As each animal is added, count the total number of animals on the flannel board as a group. For example, when the cow is added, there should be three total animals on the flannel board.

O'Brien, John, illus. *The Farmer in the Dell.*

2000. Honesdale, PA: Boyds Mills Press.

  Summary: An illustrated version of the classic song.

  Action: As you sing the song, ask children to come to the front of the room to play each of the different characters as they enter the story. Use props to signify each different character: farmer—straw hat; wife—bonnet; nurse—nurse's hat; child—baseball cap; dog—stuffed dog; cat—stuffed cat; rat—stuffed rat; cheese—plastic cheese. Have the child playing the part of the farmer hold the straw hat, the child playing the wife hold the bonnet, and so on.

Ochiltree, Dianne. *Pillow Pup.*

2002. Illus., Mireille d'Allancé. New York: Margaret K. McElderry Books.

  Summary: A playful puppy uses her little girl's pillow as a toy.

  Action: Give the children juggling scarves so they can pretend they are their pillows. When Maggie shakes the pillow from side to side, have the children shake their "pillows" around. When Maggie takes the pillow on a zig-zagging ride, have the children run in place with their "pillows." When Maggie dances, have everyone dance with their "pillows."

Odanaka, Barbara. *Smash! Mash! Crash! There Goes the Trash!*

2006. Illus., Will Hillenbrand. New York: Margaret K. McElderry Books.

  Summary: The garbage trucks make lots of noise and are fun to watch on trash day.

  Action: Before you start reading the story, put a variety of "trash" around the room. Scraps of paper are great "trash." On the fourth page, the garbage trucks make their debut in the story. At that point, bring out a trash bag and ask everyone to help the garbage trucks by putting all of the "trash" into the bag. Once the floor is clean again, continue reading the story.

Otoshi, Kathryn. *One.*

2008. San Rafael, CA: KO Kids Books.

  Summary: The color red bullies the other colors until a gray number 1 teaches them to stand up for themselves.

  Action: Give everyone six paper circles: blue, yellow, green, purple, orange, and red. As each of those colors joins the story, have everyone hold up the correct color circle.

Parker, Marjorie Blain. *Your Kind of Mommy.*

2007. Illus., Cyd Moore. New York: Dutton Children's Books.

Summary: Animals and humans have the right kind of mommies for their needs.

Action: Ask the children to bring their favorite stuffed animals or dolls to storytime. As you read the book, have them act like the various mothers in the story:

- Octopus—Give your baby a great big hug.
- Shaggy dog—Shake your bottom.
- Buzzy bee—Pretend to mix up some honey.
- Wallaby—Hold your baby close to your stomach as if you have a pouch.
- Humpback whale—Pretend to swim with your baby.
- Elephant—Hold one arm up to your face like an elephant's trunk and pretend to spray water on your baby.
- Timber wolf—Howl at the moon.

Portis, Antoinette. *Not a Stick.*

2008. New York: HarperCollins.

Summary: A pig uses his imagination and a stick to do many different things.

Action: Give everyone one rhythm stick before you start reading the book. Have the children act out the pig's imagination along with book:

- Pretend the stick is a fishing pole by pretending to cast out a line and catch a fish.
- Pretend to lead a band by marching in place and conducting the band.
- Pretend to use the stick as a paintbrush on a canvas.
- Hold the stick with two hands and pretend to lift weights.
- Hold the stick between your legs and pretend to ride a horse.
- Hold the stick to your side like a spear.
- Finally, pretend it is a sword to fight a dragon.

Puttock, Simon. *Big Bad Wolf Is Good.*

2001. Illus., Lynne Chapman. New York: Sterling.

Summary: The Big Bad Wolf decides to be good so he can make some friends.

Action: Big Bad Wolf visits three homes trying to make friends. When he visits the Goose family, the Chicken family, and the Duck family, the little birds make faces at him through the window. Use a wolf puppet or stuffed animal and have the kids make silly faces along with the baby birds.

Rao, Sandhya. *My Mother's Sari.*

2006. Illus., Nina Sabnani. New York: NorthSouth Books.

Summary: A young girl describes all the wonderful things she can do with her mother's sari.

Action: Give each child a long piece of cloth or a juggling scarf. Have the children use the cloths or scarves in a similar fashion to the way the girl uses her mother's sari:

- "My mother's sari is long like a train"—Hold up the cloth to show how long it is (you can also make a choo-choo sound if you like).
- "It fills the air with color when I dance and sing"—Sing and dance with the cloth.
- ". . . and climb up a rope"—Twist the cloth up like a rope and pretend to climb.
- "I hide with my friends"—Hold the cloth in front of your face to hide.
- "I even wipe my nose"—You probably want to skip this one.
- ". . . it wraps itself around me"—Wrap the cloth around you like a cape.
- "I sleep while it gently swings . . ."—Lay your head on the cloth like a pillow.

Redding, Sue. *Up Above and Down Below.*

2006. San Francisco: Chronicle Books.

Summary: In many environments, there are different things happening above and below the surface.

Action: Give each child a juggling scarf or a blank piece of paper. Each page refers to the activities going on above and below the surface. When you are reading about the things going on above the surface, have the children put their scarves or pieces of paper on the ground to show that they are also above the surface. When you read about things going on below the surface, have the children hold their scarves or pieces of paper above their heads.

Ries, Lori. *Super Sam!*

2004. Illus., Sue Ramá. Watertown, MA: Charlesbridge.

Summary: When Sam wears a cape, he becomes a superhero and saves the day.

Action: Give everyone a juggling scarf to use as a cape. Have the children hold the scarves over their shoulders to become superheroes like Sam:

- "Run"—Run in place with the cape.
- "Fly"—Hold the cape with one hand while you use your other arm to fly around the room.
- "Show your strength"—Hold the cape with one hand while you pretend to lift something very heavy with your other arm.
- "Leap tall buildings"—Jump up high.
- "Climb"—Hold the cape with one hand while you pretend to climb a ladder with the other arm.
- "Become invisible"—Hold the scarf over your head.
- "Escape"—Use the scarf like a cape again and run quickly in place.
- "Save the day"—Run in place for all three pages until you save the day for your younger brother.

Rohmann, Eric. *My Friend Rabbit.*

2002. Brookfield, CT: Roaring Brook Press.

Summary: When Mouse's toy plane gets stuck in a tree, Rabbit finds a unique way to retrieve it.

Action: Create a felt piece for the following animals: elephant, rhinoceros, hippopotamus, deer, alligator, bear, duck, rabbit, squirrel, and mouse. Give each animal to a different child in your program. As Rabbit piles up each animal to try to reach the plane, have the child with that animal add his or her felt piece to the flannel board. When everyone topples over, choose one child to knock all of the pieces off of the flannel board.

Root, Phyllis. *Meow Monday.*

2000. Illus., Helen Craig. Cambridge, MA: Candlewick Press.

Summary: When Bonnie Bumble's pussy willows bloom, they make so much noise that it disturbs the rest of the farm.

Action: Give everyone a die-cut cat attached to a Popsicle stick. At the end of every page, have the children hold up their cats and meow very loudly. When the pussy willows finally settle down for a catnap, the children can lay their die-cut cats on the floor for the remainder of the story.

———. *Thirsty Thursday.*

2009. Illus., Helen Craig. Somerville, MA: Candlewick Press.

Summary: On a dry summer day, Bonnie tickles a cloud with a feather to make rain.

Action: When Bonnie gathers feathers from the chickens, give everyone a fake feather (you can usually buy these at art or party supply stores). Then, when Bonnie tickles the cloud, have the children hold their feathers high up in the air and wave them around to tickle pretend clouds.

Rosenthal, Amy Krouse. *Little Oink.*

2009. Illus., Jen Corace. San Francisco: Chronicle Books.

Summary: Little Oink wants to have a clean room, but has to make a mess to be a respectable pig.

Action: Have a box of random toys ready before you start reading the story. When you get to the part where Little Oink's parents say "I still see toys in their bin, mister. Please—not another word until this room's a total pigsty," invite the children to take one toy out of your box so they can make a mess of your storytime space. Three pages later, Little Oink plays his favorite game, "House!" Invite everyone to help Little Oink clean up the mess by putting the toys back in the box.

Russo, Marisabina. *The Bunnies Are Not in Their Beds.*

2007. New York: Schwartz and Wade Books.

Summary: Mama and Daddy have to repeatedly put their active bunnies to bed.

Action: Give everyone a die-cut bunny shape attached to a Popsicle stick. Whenever the bunnies are tucked into bed, have the children lay the die-cut bunnies on the floor so they can go to sleep. Whenever you read "Mama and Daddy tiptoe up the stairs, open the door, and what do they see?" the children can pick the bunnies up off the floor and bounce them around.

Ryder, Joanne. *Dance by the Light of the Moon.*

2007. Illus., Guy Francis. New York: Hyperion Books for Children.

> **Summary:** Farmer Snow has a barnyard party so all of the animals can dance by the light of the moon.

> **Action:** Give everyone a white paper circle moon. Whenever you read about the animals dancing by the light of the moon, pause briefly so the children can dance around with their moons.

Shea, Bob. *Dinosaur vs. Bedtime.*

2008. New York: Hyperion Books for Children.

> **Summary:** Nothing can stop a little dinosaur except bedtime.

> **Action:** Give each child a die-cut dinosaur shape attached to a Popsicle stick. As dinosaur attacks each new issue, he roars and eventually wins. Each time he wins, have the children hold their dinosaurs up in the air and cheer. When he finally succumbs to sleep, the children can lay the dinosaurs on the floor.

Snyder, Betsy. *Sweet Dreams Lullaby.*

2010. New York: Random House.

> **Summary:** A young bunny goes to sleep to a soothing lullaby.

> **Action:** Ask the children to bring their favorite dolls or stuffed animals to your program. Have a couple of extra ones available in case anyone forgot. While you read the story, the kids can rock their "babies" to sleep.

Spinelli, Eileen. *Do You Have a Hat?*

2004. Illus., Geraldo Valério. New York: Simon and Schuster Books for Young Readers.

> **Summary:** A short description of many famous people who wore hats.

> **Action:** Give the children juggling scarves. Tell them to pretend the scarves are hats. On almost every page of this book, you will find the phrase "Do YOU have a hat?" When you read that line the first time, have the chil-

dren take their juggling scarves and place them on their heads like hats. After that, whenever you read that line, the children can pick the scarves up and place them back on their heads like they are tipping their hats.

Tafolla, Carmen. *What Can You Do with a Rebozo?*

2008. Illus., Amy Córdova. Berkeley, CA: Tricycle Press.

Summary: A young girl shows all of the imaginative ways she can use a rebozo, or Mexican shawl.

Action: Give every child a juggling scarf or a long piece of fabric. Have the children act like they have rebozos and play along with the young girl:

- Hold it up as if it is a butterfly and flap its "wings."
- Play peekaboo.
- Hold it on your head as if you are wrapping it in your hair.
- Wrap it around your shoulders to keep you warm.
- Use it to wipe up an imaginary spill on the floor.
- Hold it over your eyes as if you are ready to hit a piñata.
- Hold it over your head like the top of a tunnel.
- Hold it over your shoulders like a cape.
- Wrap it around your arm like a bandage.
- Finally, dance around the room with it.

Tafuri, Nancy. *The Big Storm: A Very Soggy Counting Book.*

2009. New York: Simon and Schuster Books for Young Readers.

Summary: Many different animals find shelter from the storm together, but discover that another larger animal is already using that hollow.

Action: Before the story starts, hand out a bird, mouse, squirrel, rabbit, chipmunk, woodchuck, raccoon, opossum, red fox, and skunk to some of the children in your program. You can use stuffed animals, photographs, or felt animals. As each animal enters the cozy hollow, have the child with that animal bring it up to the front of the room to place in a box. Since each animal runs for safety, everyone else can run in place while the animal is placed in the "cozy hollow." At the end when the animals notice the bears, have everyone run carefully around the room.

Trapani, Iza. *Shoo Fly!*

2000. Watertown, MA: Charlesbridge.

Summary: A mouse tries to avoid a determined fly.

Action: Give everyone a die-cut fly attached to a Popsicle stick. Every time you read the words "Shoo fly," have the children wave the fly as if it is flying away.

Van Laan, Nancy. *Scrubba Dub.*

2003. Illus., Bernadette Pons. New York: Atheneum Books for Young Readers.

Summary: Mama bunny gives her playful child a bath.

Action: Give everyone a juggling scarf at the beginning of the story. As you read the story, the children can pretend the juggling scarves are washcloths and they can wash parts of their bodies as the bunny plays in the tub.

Weeks, Sarah. *Overboard!*

2006. Illus., Sam Williams. Orlando: Harcourt.

Summary: Baby bunny likes to throw things off his highchair, out of the bath, and out of his crib.

Action: Give the children juggling scarves, or something else that they can throw in the air without hurting anyone. Every time the bunny throws something "overboard," throw the juggling scarves into the air.

Wheeler, Lisa. *Bubble Gum, Bubble Gum.*

2004. Illus., Laura Huliska-Beith. New York: Little, Brown.

Summary: A toad, shrew, goose, bee, and crow get stuck in bubble gum on the road and figure out how to escape before a truck comes along.

Action: Give everyone a piece of pink paper cut into a smooshed bubble gum shape. You can cut all of the shapes the same or cut a variety. Make sure every piece is bigger than a child's shoe. When the toad gets stuck in the bubble gum, have the children place one foot on a piece of pink paper and pretend that they are stuck. Tell them to grab their legs and pretend to try to remove their feet from the gum. Do this for each animal that gets stuck. Finally, when the animals blow a bubble to escape, everyone can remove their feet from their "bubble gum."

Whybrow, Ian. *The Noisy Way to Bed.*

2003. Illus., Tiphanie Beeke. New York: Arthur A. Levine Books.

Summary: A young boy heads to bed and meets some noisy animals along the way.

Action: Before you start reading the story, hand out a duck, horse, sheep, and pig puppet to four children in your program. When the little boy goes past the pond, meets the duck, and tells the duck he can join him, have the child with the duck puppet come to the front of the room. Continue this way with the other three animals that the little boy meets. When everyone finally goes to sleep, have the children lay their puppets down on the floor together.

Williams, Sue. *Dinnertime!*

2001. Illus., Kerry Argent. San Diego: Harcourt.

Summary: Six young rabbits escape from a hungry fox one at a time.

Action: Create six felt rabbits. Put the rabbits on your flannel board as you start the story. You will also want to hide a small basket where you can reach it, but the audience can't see it. When the fox chases the rabbits, have everyone run in place while you remove one of the rabbits from the flannel board and place it in the basket. On the page where you realize that all of the rabbits are safe at home, bring out the basket to show that your rabbits are safe as well.

Wolff, Ferida. *It Is the Wind.*

2005. Illus., James Ransome. New York: HarperCollins.

Summary: A child wonders about the sound he hears at night and finally decides it is just the wind.

Action: Give every child a juggling scarf at the beginning of the story. At the end of every page, have the children wave the scarves around in the air like the wind is blowing them. The child in the story determines that the noise is the wind on the very last page. The children in your program will enjoy knowing what the noise was all along.

Yang, James. *Joey and Jet.*

2004. New York: Atheneum Books for Young Readers.

Summary: Joey throws a ball and Jet fetches it from a long way away.

Action: Ask everyone to sit in a circle for this book. Have a couple of beach balls ready when you start to read the story. When Joey tosses the ball, toss the beach balls in the circle. Have everyone roll the balls around while you read the story. You will probably want the help of a couple of other adults to keep the balls moving while you read.

Yerrill, Gail, illus. *Starry Night, Sleep Tight: A Bedtime Book of Lullabies.*

2008. Wilton, CT: Tiger Tales.

> **Summary:** An illustrated collection of lullabies.
>
> **Action:** Ask every child to bring a favorite stuffed animal or doll to story-time. Choose one or two lullabies out of this collection to sing while the kids rock their "babies" to sleep.

Yolen, Jane, and Heidi E. Y. Stemple. *Sleep, Black Bear, Sleep.*

2007. Illus., Brooke Dyer. New York: HarperCollins.

> **Summary:** A variety of animals sleep warm and cozy when winter starts.
>
> **Action:** Hand out the following stuffed animals to children in your program: bear, frog, bat, snake, turtle, gopher, skunk, badger, beaver, mouse, toad, and chipmunk. If you don't have stuffed animals, you can use pictures or photographs of the animals instead. Put a towel or small blanket in a box that you place near your feet. As you read about each animal in the book, have the child with that animal come to the front of the room and tuck his or her stuffed animal or picture under the blanket in the box.

Zemach, Kaethe. *Just Enough and Not Too Much.*

2003. New York: Arthur A. Levine Books.

> **Summary:** When Simon decides he wants more chairs, hats, and toys, he discovers that there isn't enough room in his house.
>
> **Action:** Before the story begins, give every child one of the following: a dollhouse chair (or picture of a chair), a hat (or a hat made out of paper), or a trinket toy. Ask the other people you work with for help if you can't find enough supplies. Also, have a small box that is barely big enough to fit everything you have handed out. When Simon gets a bunch of chairs, have all of the children with chairs come up and add them to your box. Do the same with the hats and the toys. Then show everyone how crowded the box is before you continue reading the story.

more storytime resources

Baltuck, Naomi. *Storytime Stretchers.* *2007. Atlanta: August House.*
This resource is full of activities that involve audience participation in between books. There are jokes, tongue twisters, songs, and stories. Any of these ideas can be used to make a more interactive storytime.

Bauer, Caroline Feller. *Leading Kids to Books through Crafts.* *2000. Chicago: American Library Association.*
This resource has directions for easy, child-friendly crafts. After each craft, there are poems, stories, rhymes, and books suitable for the theme.

Bromann, Jennifer. *Storytime Action! 2000+ Ideas for Making 500 Picture Books Interactive.* *2003. New York: Neal-Schuman.*
The title says it all. This resource includes many ideas for interaction between the audience and the picture book. Some of the activities include movement; some involve asking questions of the children. This resource is great if you wish to find ideas for books written prior to 2000.

Cullum, Carolyn N. *The Storytime Sourcebook: A Compendium of Ideas and Resources for Storytellers.* *1999. 2nd ed. New York: Neal-Schuman.*
This resource is great for someone just starting to do storytime or someone who needs some new program themes. It includes videos, books,

fingerplays, crafts, activities, and songs for 146 different storytime top-
ics. From this information, librarians or teachers can create their own
storytimes with interaction in between the stories read.

Faurot, Kimberly K. *Books in Bloom: Creative Patterns and Props
That Bring Stories to Life.* *2003. Chicago: American Library Association.*
This resource includes a variety of ideas on how the storyteller can use
puppets and other props to enhance storytelling. There are also patterns
for creating the props.

Lincycomb, Kay. *Storytimes . . . Plus!* *2007. New York: Neal-Schuman.*
This resource provides "complete, ready to use, storytimes" (p. xi). There
are fantastic rhymes, activities, and crafts to use in storytimes. Many
books are also listed for each theme.

MacDonald, Margaret Read. *Shake-It-Up Tales!* *2000. Little Rock, AR:
August House.*
This resource provides a variety of stories that invite audience participation and movement. This is a great book for someone who wants to
include more of the oral tradition in their programming.

Nespeca, Sue McCleaf, and Joan B. Reeve. *Picture Books Plus.* *2003.
Chicago: American Library Association.*
Art, drama, music, math, and science extension activities are provided
for picture books for preschoolers through third graders. These activities can be used after reading the books.

Raines, Shirley C., and Robert J. Canady. *Story S-T-R-E-T-C-H-E-R-S.*
1989. Beltsville, MD: Gryphon House.
This resource shows five activities or ideas to "stretch" each book after
you finish reading it.

Reid, Rob. *Something Musical Happened at the Library: Adding
Song and Dance to Children's Story Programs.* *2007. Chicago: American Library Association.*
This is a great resource for ideas of songs to use in between the books
in your programs. The first chapter contains eight story programs with
books and accompanying songs. The next five chapters include lists of

songs matched with picture books, musical ideas, and other songs. The final chapter includes a wonderful list of books based on songs, music, or dance.

Reid, Rob. *Shake and Shout: 16 Noisy, Lively Story Programs.* *2008. Janesville, WI: Upstart Books.*

Much like *Storytimes . . . Plus!* this resource provides fully developed storytimes. The storytimes include a lot of movement through rhymes, songs, and books.

art outlines

contents

apple

bear

bed

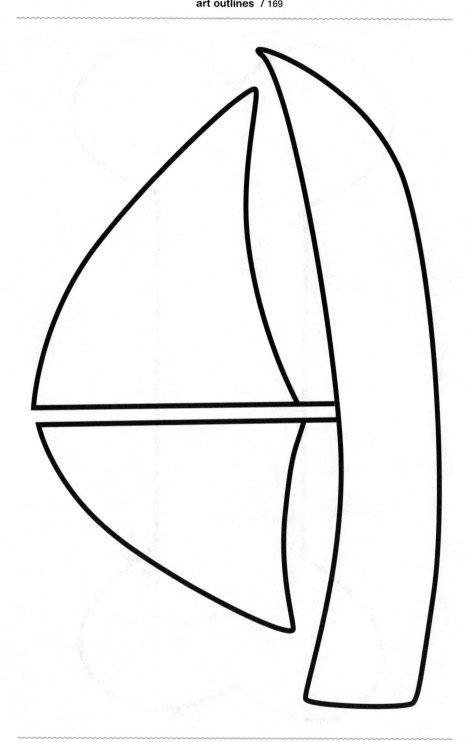

boat

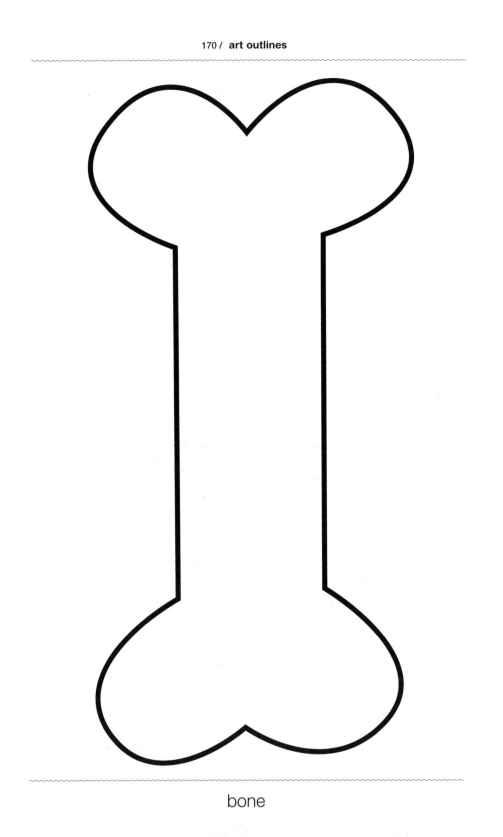

bone

butterfly

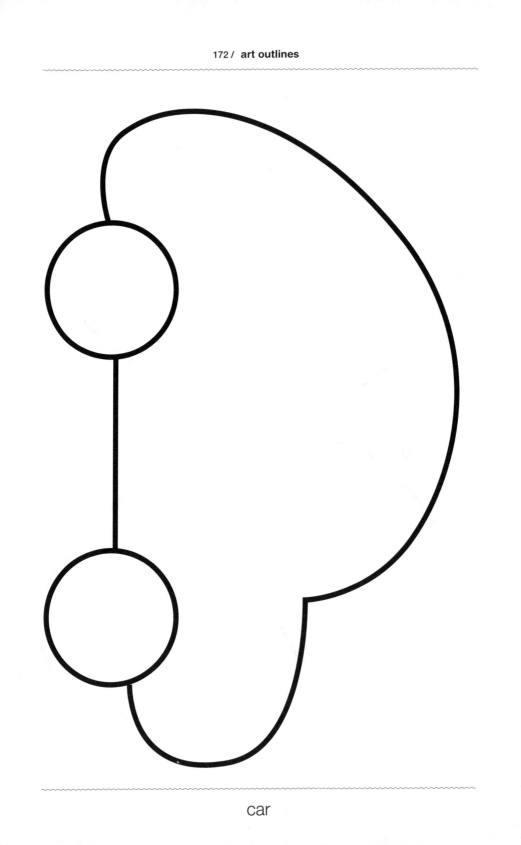

car

cat

cloud

COW

cowboy hat and eye patch

cupcake

dog

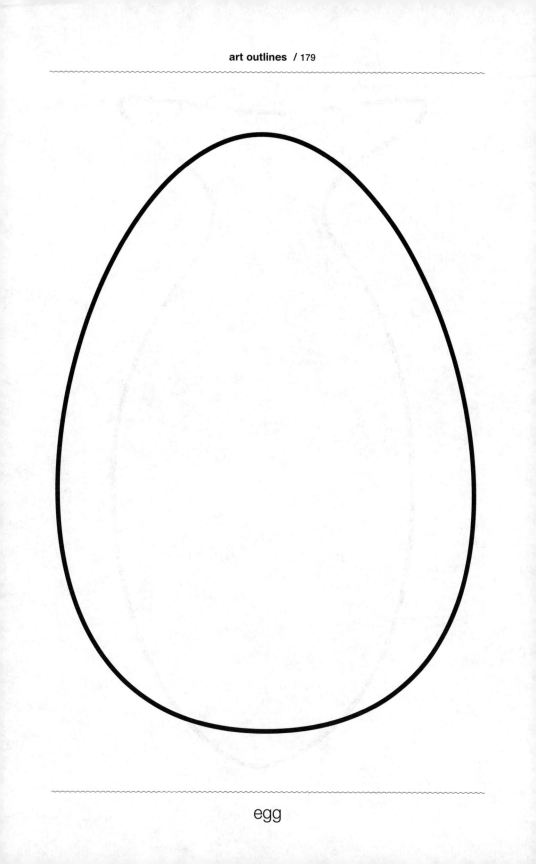

egg

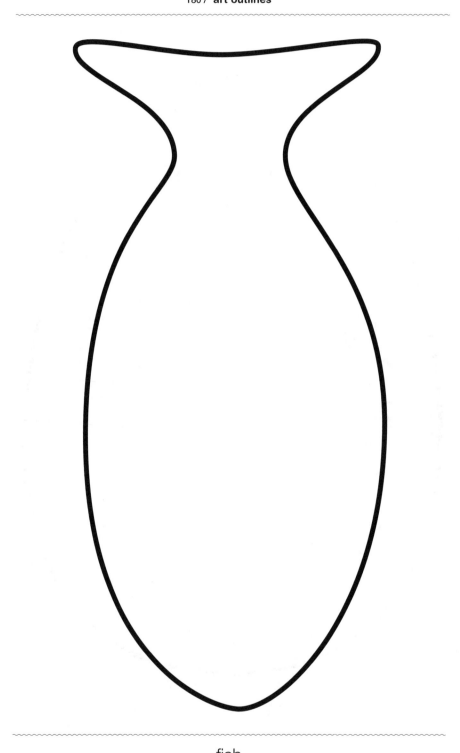

fish

flamingo

heart

house

penguin

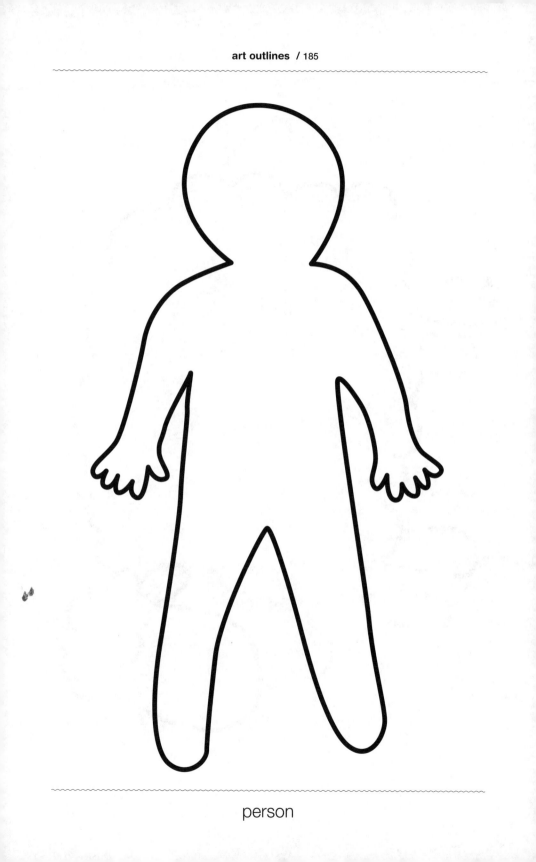

person

sheep

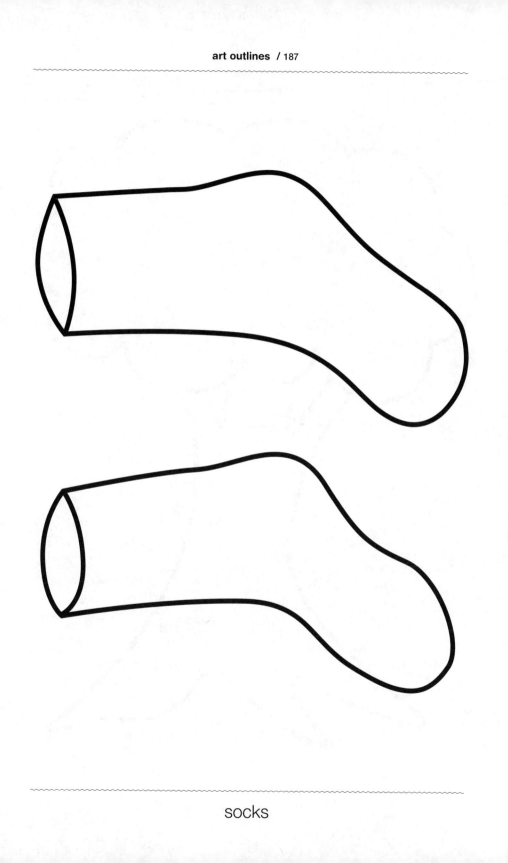

socks

tree

window

author index

title index

subject index

worms

See insects

Z

zoos